Lego Mindstorms™ NXT 2.0 for Teens

Jerry Lee Ford, Jr.

Course Technology PTR

A part of Cengage Learning

COURSE TECHNOLOGY
CENGAGE Learning™

Australia • Brazil • Japan • Korea • Mexico • Singapore • Spain • United Kingdom • United States

COURSE TECHNOLOGY
CENGAGE Learning™

Lego Mindstorms™ NXT 2.0 for Teens
Jerry Lee Ford, Jr.

**Publisher and General Manager,
Course Technology PTR:** Stacy L. Hiquet

Associate Director of Marketing:
Sarah Panella

Manager of Editorial Services:
Heather Talbot

Marketing Manager: Jordan Castellani

Senior Acquisitions Editor: Emi Smith

Project Editor: Jenny Davidson

Copyeditor: Sandy Doell

Technical Reviewer: JT Hiquet

Interior Layout Tech: MPS Limited, a Macmillan Company

Cover Designer: Mike Tanamachi

Indexer: Sharon Shock

For product information and technology assistance, contact us at
Cengage Learning Customer & Sales Support, 1-800-354-9706

For permission to use material from this text or product,
submit all requests online at **www.cengage.com/permissions**
Further permissions questions can be emailed to
permissionrequest@cengage.com

Lego Mindstorms is a trademark of the LEGO Group. All other trademarks are the property of their respective owners.

All images © Cengage Learning unless otherwise noted.

Library of Congress Control Number: 2009933328

ISBN-13: 978-1-4354-5480-4

ISBN-10: 1-4354-5480-4

Course Technology, a part of Cengage Learning
20 Channel Center Street
Boston, MA 02210
USA

Cengage Learning is a leading provider of customized learning solutions with office locations around the globe, including Singapore, the United Kingdom, Australia, Mexico, Brazil, and Japan. Locate your local office at: **international.cengage.com/region**

Cengage Learning products are represented in Canada by Nelson Education, Ltd.

For your lifelong learning solutions, visit **courseptr.com**

Visit our corporate website at **cengage.com**

Printed by RR Donnelley. Crawfordsville, IN. 1st Ptg. 12/2010

Printed in the United States of America
1 2 3 4 5 6 7 12 11 10

To my wonderful children, Alexander, William, and Molly,
and my beautiful wife, Mary.

ACKNOWLEDGMENTS

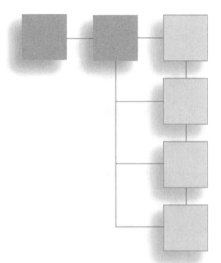

This book represents the hard work of a number of talented individuals to whom I owe a great many thanks. For starters I want to thank Emi Smith, who as acquisitions editor, helped make this book a reality. I especially need to express my gratitude to Jenny Davidson, who served as this book's project editor. As she has demonstrated so many times in the past, Jenny's guidance and editorial skills were essential to the success of this book. Thanks also go out to this book's technical editor, JT Hiquet, for providing invaluable insights and technical advice and to Sandy Doell, who served as the book's copyeditor. Lastly, I'd be remiss if I did not remember to thank all the people working behind the scenes at Course Technology PTR for all their contributions and hard work.

About the Author

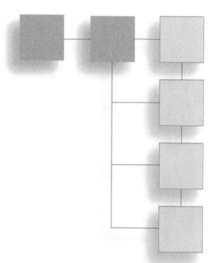

Jerry Lee Ford, Jr. is an author, educator, and an IT professional with over 21 years of experience in information technology, including roles as an automation analyst, technical manager, technical support analyst, automation engineer, and security analyst. He is the author of 36 books and co-author of two additional books. His published works include *Getting Started with Game Maker*, *DarkBASIC Programming for the Absolute Beginner*, *Scratch Programming for Teens*, *Microsoft Visual Basic 2008 Express Programming for the Absolute Beginner*, and *Phrogram Programming for the Absolute Beginner*. Jerry has a master's degree in business administration from Virginia Commonwealth University in Richmond, Virginia, and he has over five years of experience as an adjunct instructor teaching networking courses in information technology.

CONTENTS

INTRODUCTION

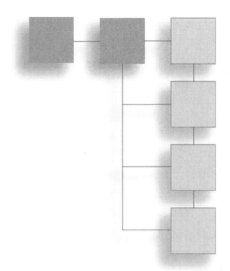

Welcome to *Lego Mindstorms NXT 2.0 for Teens*! Lego Mindstorms NXT 2.0 is a programmable robotics kit made by Lego. Lego Mindstorms NXT 2.0 is the latest version of this kit, released in August 2009. The kit is made up of a micro-computer, electronic motors and sensors, as well as various Lego bricks and Lego Technic pieces like beams, axles, and gears, 619 pieces in total.

The Lego Mindstorms NXT 2.0 kit comes equipped with everything you need to build all sorts of robotic creations. It includes a software programming language called NXT-G, which is used to write the programs that are downloaded into your robotic creations in order to bring them to life. NXT-G is an icon-based, drag-and-drop language, which means that there is no complex programming language that must be mastered.

Until the advent of Lego Mindstorms, robotic development was the realm in which only an exclusive group of highly educated and technically proficient engineers and programmers were able to play. Lego Mindstorms NXT 2.0 changes all that. Lego Mindstorms NXT 2.0 provides you with a complete framework for robotic development. It does not require you to have an advanced degree in computer science in order to use it. This book will provide you with everything you need to know in order to get up and running with Lego Mindstorms NXT 2.0 and NXT-G.

By following along with this book's step-by-step, hands-on instruction, you will learn how to create all sorts of robotic creations and to develop the program code that will make them work. Although Lego Mindstorms NXT 2.0 comes in both retail and an education kit, this book will focus on robotic development using the retail kit (set number 8527). This kit is available for purchase at www.lego.com or at your local TOYS 'R US store. It costs around $280. The educational kit (set number 9797) is almost identical to the retail kit, except that it includes a few additional components.

WHY LEGO MINDSTORMS NXT 2.0?

Lego Mindstorms is named after a book titled *Mindstorms: Children, Computer, and Power Ideas* published in 1993. Lego Mindstorms NXT 2.0 was released on August 1, 2009. Together, Lego Mindstorms NXT 2.0 and NXT-G provide you with everything you need to create just about anything you can imagine. Robot creation is a three-step process. First you use Lego bricks to create your robot. Then you use NXT-G to write the program code that makes your creations work. Then you download the program code into the NXT Brick, a small micro-computer that is the brain of your creations, and then step back and watch them come alive.

Lego Mindstorms NXT 2.0/NXT-G software runs on Microsoft Windows or Mac OS X. It is easy to install and learn. You can download your program code into your creations using a USB cable. If your computer has Bluetooth installed, you can use it to wirelessly download your program code. Examples of the types of creations you can build include things like:

- Robots that move, see, and react to their environment

- Different types of vehicles (cars, tanks, etc.)

- Robotic arms like those used in manufacturing plants

- A robotic warning system that alerts you when someone enters your room

- Robotic animals that move and act like their real-life counterparts

Of course, Lego Mindstorms NXT 2.0 doesn't limit you to the types of robotic creations listed above. You can use it to create pretty much anything you can imagine.

Who Should Read this Book?

Lego Mindstorms NXT 2.0 for Teens has been designed to meet the needs of anyone interested in learning about robotic development using Lego Mindstorms NXT 2.0. As this book will show you, building your own robotic creations is a lot of fun. It's a lot more fun than any robot toy you can buy. This book will not only teach you the basic principles behind good robotic design but will also give you a solid understanding of the programming principles involved in the creation of NXT-G programs. By the time you are done with this book, you will have learned how to create all sorts of cool projects.

Lego Mindstorms NXT 2.0 is easy enough for kids as young as 10 years old to learn while at the same time is powerful to meet the needs of adults and advanced robotic hobbyists. It provides everything you will need to complete even the most advanced robotic project, including a powerful microcomputer, servo motors, and a variety of sensors that can detect color, light, movement, distance, and touch. Software features include editors that let you download and play sound files on the NXT Brick as well as an image editor that you can use to create graphics and display them on the NXT Brick's LCD. There is even a remote control application that you can use to control your robots.

While previous robotic development and programming experience is helpful, it is not a requirement of this book. You only need have a good understanding of either Microsoft Windows or Mac OS X to get started. If you know how to operate a computer and are comfortable working with applications like Microsoft Office, you'll be surprised how quickly you will pick things up.

Advanced robotic developers, on the other hand, will be happy to learn that Lego Mindstorms NXT 2.0's development framework provides everything required to develop advanced projects. As such, it is a great tool for quickly building and testing prototypes. It can be used to create stand-alone robots or robots that are designed to interact with other robots. You can even use certain Bluetooth-enabled telephones to interact with and control your robots. All you need to get up and running quickly is Lego Mindstorms NXT 2.0 and this book. In no time at all, you will be building and playing with all kinds of robots and mechanized systems and models.

WHAT YOU NEED TO BEGIN

As I mentioned, Lego Mindstorms NXT 2.0 comes in two versions, a retail version that sells for around $280 and an education set. The education set contains everything that the retail version has plus a few additional components. This book is based on the retail version, although the education set can be used if that's what you have.

The Lego Mindstorms NXT 2.0 kit comes with everything you need to get started except for a computer, which you will need to develop programs for your projects. Although there are dozens of third-party programming languages with varying levels of complexity that can be used, NXT-G is arguably the simplest and easiest to learn and is the programming language used throughout this book.

The Lego Mindstorms NXT 2.0 software will run on any of the following versions of Microsoft Windows.

- Windows XP with Service Pack 2 (Home Edition, Professional)

- Windows Vista with Service Pack 1

- Windows 7

In addition, the Lego Mindstorms NXT 2.0 software will also run on all of the following versions of Mac OS X.

- Mac OS X 10.3

- Mac OS X 10.4

- Mac OS X 10.5

Although various versions of Microsoft Windows and Mac OS X are supported, this book will demonstrate the execution of NXT-G software on a system running Windows Vista. Regardless of which operating systems you use, the steps you follow and the program code that is generated is the same.

In order to install and operate Lego Mindstorms NXT 2.0 on a Microsoft Windows system, your computer must meet the minimum hardware requirements listed in the following table. However, for good performance, you will want to make sure that your computer exceeds these requirements.

Minimum Requirements for Lego Mindstorms NXT 2.0 on Windows

Resource	Minimum Requirement
Processor	1 GHz Intel (1.5 GHz recommended)
Memory	512 MB
Hard Disk	700 MB
CD-ROM	Any speed
Display	XGA (1024 × 768)
USB Port	1
Bluetooth Adapter	Optional

If, on the other hand, your computer runs on Mac OS X, it must meet the following requirements.

Minimum Requirements for Lego Mindstorms NXT 2.0 on Mac OS X

Resource	Minimum Requirement
Processor	PowerPC G3, G4, G5, 600 MHz Intel (1.3 GHz recommended)
Memory	512 MB
Hard Disk	700 MB
CD-ROM	Any speed
Display	XGA (1024 × 768)
USB Port	1
Bluetooth Adapter	Optional

Assuming your Microsoft Windows or Mac OS X computer meets the hardware and software requirements previously outlined, all you need to get started developing your own robotic creations is the Lego Mindstorms NXT 2.0 kit and this book. It won't take long before you will be creating all kinds of exciting robots, mechanized systems, and models.

CONVENTIONS USED IN THIS BOOK

This book uses a number of conventions in order to make it easier for you to read and work with the information that is provided. These conventions are as follows.

Hint

Tips for doing things differently and things that you can do to become a more proficient robotic developer.

Trap

Areas where problems are likely to occur and advice on how to stay away from or deal with those problems, hopefully saving you the pain of learning about them on your own the hard way.

Trick

Shortcuts designed to help make you a better and more efficient robotic developer.

CD-ROM Downloads

If you purchased an ebook version of this book, and the book had a companion CD-ROM, you may download the contents from www.courseptr.com/downloads.

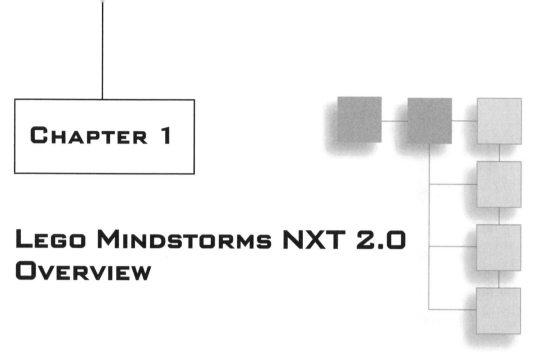

CHAPTER 1

LEGO MINDSTORMS NXT 2.0 OVERVIEW

No so long ago robotic development was limited to the realm of engineers, advanced programmers, and highly skilled machinists. While robotic development was frequently used in manufacturing and other high-end technical fields, those who built robots as a hobby had to be very creative and resourceful. Not only did they have to figure out how to design their own robots, but they also had to build and create their parts. Lego Mindstorms NXT 2.0 greatly simplifies things by providing you with prebuilt Lego components that provide a framework specifically designed for building robots. So there is no more soldering, no more wiring, and no more jury rigging.

This chapter provides you with a high-level overview of Lego Mindstorms NXT 2.0. The major topics covered in this chapter include:

- A review of Lego Mindstorms origins
- A high level overview of the components that make up the Lego Mindstorms NXT 2.0 kit
- Learning about the three steps involved in building robots
- Learning how to install the Lego Mindstorms NXT 2.0 software
- Learning about the Lego Mindstorms NXT community

Lego Mindstorms Origins

In 1998 Lego introduced the world to the Robotics Invention System, or RIS. This kit consisted of a pair of motors, two touch sensors, and a light sensor. The kit also included a microcomputer called the RCX, which provided a brain for robotic creations, executing programs downloaded from a Windows or Mac OS X computer via an infrared interface. The RCX featured a small LCD, which could be used to view and interact with the device. Initially the RCX was powered by a power adapter. Later versions liberated robotic creations by replacing the power adapter with batteries.

The first version of Lego Mindstorms NXT was released in 2006. Lego named this new robotic kit Mindstorms NXT based on a book titled *Mindstorms: Children, Computers, and Powerful Ideas*. The first version contained 619 Technic pieces, an ultrasonic sensor, sound sensor, touch sensor, and a light sensor as well as three servo motors, and it included the NXT-G programming language.

Hint

If you want to learn more about the Robotics Invention System and the previous version of Lego Mindstorms NXT, visit http://en.wikipedia.org/wiki/Robotics_Invention_System and http://en.wikipedia.org/wiki/Lego_Mindstorms_NXT.

Lego Mindstorms NXT 2.0 was released by Lego in August 2009. Though similar to the previous version, a number of major improvements were made, and some pieces were changed. The version 2.0 set no longer comes with a sound sensor or a light sensor. Instead, it has two touch sensors and a new color sensor. The color sensor supports three functions. Not only can it detect different colors, but it can also serve as both a lamp and a light sensor. In addition, the Mindstorms NXT 2.0 software has been enhanced. It now has new sound and image editors and a remote control application.

The sound editor allows you to convert sound files on your computer into a format supported by the NXT Brick and then to download them. Downloaded sound files can be played through the NXT Brick's built-in speaker. This way you can make your robots play all kinds of sound effects or even talk. The image editor lets you convert and download graphic files onto your NXT, where they can then be loaded and displayed on the brick's LCD screen. The remote control application allows you to control your robotic creations from your computer. On top of all this, there is a new packaging tool that helps make sharing NXT-G programs a lot easier.

Hint

If you are feeling nostalgic, you can purchase the Robotics Invention System online via eBay for roughly the same price that the Mindstorms NXT 2.0 kit sells for today.

GETTING TO KNOW LEGO MINDSTORMS NXT 2.0

The Lego Mindstorms NXT 2.0 kit consists of numerous components. These components provide a sophisticated framework that is specifically designed to support the development of robots and other sorts of mechanized creations. This framework consists of several different components, including:

- The Lego Mindstorms NXT 2.0 kit's brick, motors, sensors, and Lego bricks
- The Lego Mindstorms NXT software
- The NXT-G programming language

Together, these components provide you with everything needed to build just about anything you can imagine.

The Lego Mindstorms NXT 2.0 Kit's Brick, Motors, Sensors, and Lego Bricks

While the Lego Mindstorms NXT 2.0 kit consists of 619 pieces, the heart of your robotic creations consists of a handful of key electronic components. Figure 1.1 identifies and depicts each of these components.

The servo motors and the sensors are connected to the NXT Brick by way of small six-wire cables. These cables carry bi-directional communication between the NXT Brick and the electronic components. The NXT microcomputer, usually referred to as the NXT Brick or NXT, is the brain of your robotic creations. Compared to modern computers of today, the NXT Brick is not a very powerful computer. However, it is perfectly well designed and suited for its task, which is to run small, efficient programs and to communicate with and power its servo motors and sensors.

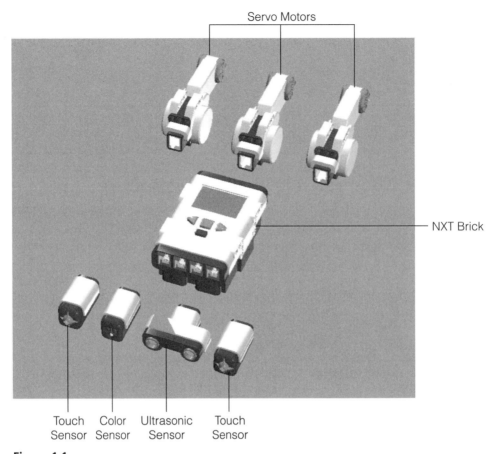

Figure 1.1
The NXT Brick, servo motors, and sensors make up the heart of your robotic creations.

The Lego Mindstorms NXT 2.0 kit also consists of a large collection of Lego pieces, including gears, beams, pegs, axles, and so on, as depicted in Figure 1.2.

The Lego Mindstorms NXT Software

Just as important as the various pieces and parts supplied with the Mindstorms NXT 2.0 set is the software that ties everything together. This includes both the Integrated Development Environment (IDE), shown in Figure 1.3, which you will learn to work with when developing programs for your robotic creations as well as the NXT-G programming language with which those programs are written.

Figure 1.2
An example of the many different types of pieces included in the Lego Mindstorms NXT 2.0 kit.

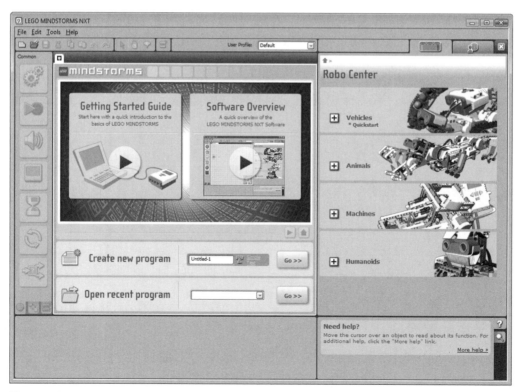

Figure 1.3
The Mindstorms NXT 2.0 IDE consists of an assortment of different specialized windows.

Hint

You will learn more about the Mindstorms NXT 2.0 IDE in Chapter 2, "Getting Started."

Using the IDE, you can create and edit NXT-G programs and download them to your NXT Brick. In addition, the IDE contains features like the Robo Center window, which provides easy access to building instructions for creating different types of robots and the My Portal window that provides access to all kinds of online resources and helps Mindstorms NXT developers to stay in touch with the latest happenings in the Mindstorms NXT community.

The software also includes an editor that allows you to record sounds on your computer that can then be used by programs in the NXT Brick and an editor that can be used to create, edit, and download graphics to the NXT Brick.

The NXT-G Programming Language

NXT-G is the official programming language provided by Lego for use with Mindstorms NXT. It is automatically installed on your computer when you install the Lego Mindstorms NXT software, so it is readily available to you. As demonstrated in Figure 1.4, the NXT-G programming language consists of a

Figure 1.4
NXT-G programs consist of various combinations of program blocks.

series of programming blocks. NXT programs are created by dragging, dropping, and snapping together these code blocks. Because of this, it is easier to learn than the many other NXT-compatible programming languages.

Compared to other compatible Mindstorms NXT programming languages, NXT-G programs tend to be larger and take up more storage space. They also take longer to download. However, the trade-off is usually well worth it, especially if you are a first time robotic developer who does not want to get bogged down in learning the fundamentals of computer programming before you can begin developing robotic creations.

NXT-G programs are developed on your Windows or Mac OS X computer, but they are designed to be executed by the NXT Brick, providing the instructions that make your robotic creations move, talk, sense, and react to their environment.

INSTALLING THE MINDSTORMS NXT 2.0 SOFTWARE

The Mindstorms NXT 2.0 software works on both Microsoft Windows and Mac OS X. Before you try installing Mindstorms NXT 2.0, make sure your computer meets the minimum system requirements, which were outlined in the book's Introduction.

Installing Mindstorms NXT 2.0 Software on Microsoft Windows

Before installing Mindstorms NXT 2.0 on Microsoft Windows, make sure that you close any currently open programs. You can then complete the installation by executing the following procedure.

Step-by-Step

1. Insert the Lego Mindstorms NXT 2.0 CD-ROM into your computer's CD-ROM drive.

2. The window shown in Figure 1.5 should appear within a few moments. If it does not, locate the autorun.exe file on the CD-ROM and double click on it. Select your preferred language.

3. Click on Allow if prompted for permission to run the setup.exe program.

Figure 1.5
Beginning the installation procedure for Lego Mindstorms NXT 2.0 on Microsoft Windows.

4. The next window that appears specifies the features being installed and the directory into which the application files are to be copied. Click on Next to accept the default settings.

5. The Lego Mindstorms NXT Software license agreement is displayed next. Review the terms of the agreement and then click on the I accept the License Agreements(s) option and click on Next.

6. Installation summary information is then displayed, identifying the changes about to be made. Click on Next to continue the installation process.

7. Over the next several minutes, the Lego Mindstorms NXT 2.0 application files are copied onto your computer. Once complete, you'll see a window prompting you to view the application's Readme file and to register the software with Lego.

Hint

You can view the Readme file at any time by clicking on Start > All Programs > Lego Mindstorms NXT 2.0 > Read Me. You can register your copy of the software any time by clicking on Help > Register Product.

8. Click on Finish to complete the installation procedure.

Once installed, you can start Mindstorms NXT 2.0 by clicking on Start > All Programs > Lego Mindstorms NXT 2.0 > Lego Mindstorms NXT 2.0.

Installing Mindstorms NXT 2.0 on Mac OS X

Before installing Mindstorms NXT 2.0 on a Mac OS X computer, make sure that you close any currently open programs. You can then complete the installation by executing the following procedure.

Step-by-Step

1. Insert the Lego Mindstorms NXT 2.0 CD-ROM into your computer's CD-ROM drive.

2. Locate and open the Mindstorms NXT folder and double click on the Install file.

3. The Lego Mindstorms NXT v2.0 window appears. Select your preferred language.

4. A window appears welcoming you to the install program. Click on Continue.

5. The Lego Mindstorms Read Me file is displayed. Review its content and then click on Continue.

6. The Lego Mindstorms NXT Software license agreement is displayed. Review its content and then click on Continue.

7. When prompted, click on Agree to accept the terms of the license agreement.

8. You are then prompted to specify the location where you wish to install the application. After specifying an appropriate location, click on Continue.

9. Click on Install to begin the install process.

10. If prompted, supply a password and click on OK in order to continue the installation.

11. Over the next several minutes, the Lego Mindstorms NXT 2.0 application files are copied onto your computer. Once this has completed, you'll see a window prompting you to restart your computer. Click on Restart.

Once installed, you can start Mindstorms NXT 2.0, as shown in Figure 1.6, by opening the Applications folder followed by the Lego Mindstorms NXT subfolder and then double clicking on the Mindstorms NXT icon.

Figure 1.6
Mindstorms NXT 2.0 on Mac OS X looks, feels, and operates very much the same as it does on Microsoft Windows.

THE THREE STEPS IN BUILDING ROBOTS

No matter how simple or complex your project may be, there are three high-level steps involved in the creation of every NXT robot. These steps are outlined in the following list:

1. Building the robot

2. Programming the robot

3. Activating the robot

Of course, every robotic project is different and there will be variations in the manner that each of these steps is performed.

Building Robots

The first step in building a new robot is to sit down and build it. One way of going about this is to build the robot based on a set of existing building instructions. The Mindstorms NXT 2.0 set comes with a Quick Start Guide that walks you through the creation of a robotic vehicle. The Mindstorms NXT software's Robo Center includes instructions for creating four additional robots. Instructions for building additional robots can be found online at http://mindstorms.lego.com. You will also find detailed instructions for building several robots in this book. Last but not least, you can use your own imagination to build anything you can think of.

Developing NXT-G Programs

In order to breathe life into your robots, you need to develop and then download a software program that tells the NXT Brick what you want it to do. If you create a robot based on online instructions downloaded from the Internet, you may be able to download a software program for it. In addition, you will find instructions for developing the program files for all of the robotic projects presented in this book. Of course, you will have to learn how to develop your own program files for any robots that you create on your own.

Writing NXT-G Programs

The Mindstorms NXT 2.0 software and NXT-G programming language provide everything you need to create software programs that bring robots to life. NXT-G is a unique programming language. There are no complicated syntax requirements that you must follow. There is no laundry list of keywords or language elements to learn. Instead, you create NXT-G programs by dragging and dropping and then configuring different types of programming blocks. Figure 1.7 shows an example of a simple NXT-G program file.

Program icons are located on the left side of the Mindstorms NXT 2.0 GUI. Each program icon performs a specific function. They can be used to control servo motor movement, display messages, collect and process sensor input, play sounds, and more. Using a combination of program blocks, you can make your robots do whatever you wish.

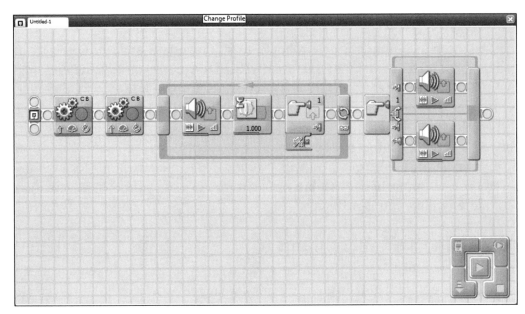

Figure 1.7
NXT-G programs consist of various combinations of program blocks that are configured to perform specific tasks.

Sidebar

NXT-G may be the programming language that Lego supplies with the Lego Mindstorms NXT 2.0 kit, but it is only one of many programming languages that support NXT program development. The following is a partial listing of NXT-compatible programming languages.

- RobotC—http://www.robotc.net

- Ruby-nxt—http://rubyforge.org/projects/ruby-nxt/

- pbLua—http://www.hempeldesigngroup.com/lego/pbLua/

- Lego:NXT—http://search.cpan.org/~collins/LEGO-NXT-2.00-1/

- Lego.NET—http://www.dcl.hpi.uni-potsdam.de/research/lego.NET/

- NXT++—http://nxtpp.clustur.com/

- RoboRealm—http://www.roborealm.com/

- SqLego—http://wiki.squeak.org/squeak/2412

- NXT_Python—http://code.google.com/p/nxt-python/

For a more complete list of available programming languages, visit http://en.wikipedia.org/wiki/Lego_Mindstorms.

Downloading Program Code

Once you have your NXT-G program working like you want it to, you must download it into the NXT Brick in order to make your robot come alive. You can do so using a USB connection between your computer and NXT Brick. The Lego Mindstorms NXT 2.0 kit includes a USB cable. Alternatively, if your computer has Bluetooth capability, you can use it to wirelessly download your NXT-G programs.

Hint

The NXT Bricks can use Bluetooth to upload programs and files from your computer. NXT Bricks have an approximate range of 33 feet (10m). In addition, you can use it to establish wireless communication with other Bluetooth-enabled devices, including Bluetooth-enabled cell phones or other NXT robots.

This book will explain how to use the Lego Mindstorms 2.0 kit's USB cable to establish communication between the NXT Brick and the computer. If your computer has Bluetooth capability and you want to use that instead, refer to the Lego Mindstorms User Guide supplied as part of the Lego Mindstorms NXT 2.0 kit for detailed instructions on how to work with it.

Activating Your Robots

The last step in the development of a robot, once you have created it and its program file and then downloaded that file into the NXT Brick, is to activate your robot. This is where the rubber meets the road and the fun really begins as you watch what you've built spring into action. Activating a NXT robot is usually as easy as pressing a NXT Brick button and putting your robotic creation down on the floor or table top.

JOINING THE LEGO MINDSTORMS COMMUNITY

Although there are many web sites dedicated to Lego Mindstorms NXT, the Lego Mindstorms web site located at http://mindstorms.lego.com, shown in Figure 1.8, represents the heart and soul of the Lego Mindstorms Community, which consists of an estimated 400,000 plus Mindstorms robotic enthusiasts around the world. The web site is designed to facilitate community collaboration, facilitating project sharing, development contests, and various other events.

Figure 1.8
The Lego Mindstorms web site is the focal point of all activity within the user community.

Figure 1.9
The FIRST LEGO League provides a great platform for young people to get involved in the Lego Mindstorms Community.

The Lego Mindstorms community is a very active group. In addition to the Lego Mindstorms web site, there are many other web sites and organizations dedicated to Lego development. One such group is the FIRST LEGO League or FLL. The FLL, shown in Figure 1.9, is a worldwide robotic design competition started in 1999 for the purpose of getting children interested in science and technology. The FLL has grown in popularity to include over 140,000 people in 56 countries around the world. To learn more about it visit http://www. firstlegoleague.org.

Hint

See Appendix B for a listing of other web sites dedicated to Lego Mindstorms development.

Summary

As this chapter explained, thanks to the Lego Mindstorms NXT 2.0 kit, robotic development is no longer the exclusive domain of large companies and advanced machinists, engineers, and programmers. This chapter provided you with an overview of Lego Mindstorms NXT 2.0, covering its history, major components, and the three steps involved in building robots. You learned how to install Lego Mindstorms NXT 2.0 on both Windows and Mac OS X computers. You also learned about the Lego Community and the FIRST LEGO League.

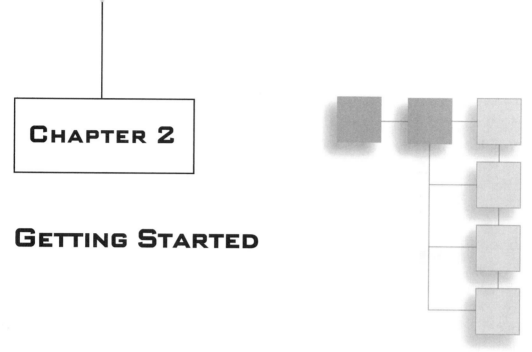

CHAPTER 2

GETTING STARTED

In Chapter 1, "Lego Mindstorms NXT 2.0 Overview," you were introduced to Lego Mindstorms NXT 2.0. This included a review of its history and major components. You also learned how to install the Mindstorms NXT 2.0 software on both Microsoft Windows and Mac OS X. Now it is time to learn about the Mindstorms NXT 2.0 graphical user interface, which you must fully understand so you can master Lego robotic development and create the software programs that will bring your robotic creations to life. By the time you finish this chapter, you will have a solid understanding of the Mindstorms NXT 2.0 GUI and will learn how to create and execute your first NXT-G program.

The major topics covered in this chapter include:

- A review of all of the major windows and components that make up the NXT 2.0 GUI
- Learning how to create your first NXT program
- Learning how to connect your NXT Brick to your computer
- Learning how to download your NXT-G program to your NXT Brick
- Learning how to execute your NXT-G programs

NAVIGATING THE MINDSTORMS NXT 2.0 GUI

The Mindstorms NXT 2.0 graphical user interface, or GUI, is a powerful and complex tool that provides you with everything you need to develop software programs using the NXT-G programming language and then download them into your NXT Brick. A good understanding of the menus, toolbar, and windows that make up this interface is essential to any Mindstorms developer.

Examining the NXT 2.0 GUI

The primary Mindstorms NXT 2.0 window consists of a menu bar, toolbar, and various other features as shown in Figure 2.1. This window is reached by starting Lego Mindstorms NXT 2.0 and then clicking on File > New. Additional features and functionality are made available through various other windows, which are accessible from the menu bar and NXT Controller.

Each of the GUI components shown in Figure 2.1 is examined more fully throughout the rest of this chapter.

Accessing NXT 2.0 Functionality via Keyboard Shortcuts

In addition to accessing and executing commands by way of the Mindstorms NXT 2.0 GUI's menu, toolbar, and windows, you can access commonly used commands and resources using NXT 2.0 keyboard shortcuts. A complete listing of these shortcuts, many of which are also visible on Mindstorms NXT 2.0 menus, is provided in Table 2.1.

The Menu Bar

The Mindstorms NXT 2.0 menu bar provides access to commands and windows that perform an assortment of tasks. It is organized into four primary menus: File, Edit, Tools, and Help as shown in Figure 2.2.

The File menu contains commands that allow you to create, open, close, and save programs. Commands are also available to print out a visual diagram of your programs and to exit the application.

The Edit menu contains commands that allow you to undo and redo program changes and to copy, cut, paste, and clear program icons. Commands are also available that let you create and edit custom blocks. Other available commands

Menu bar   Toolbar   Robo Center   My Portal

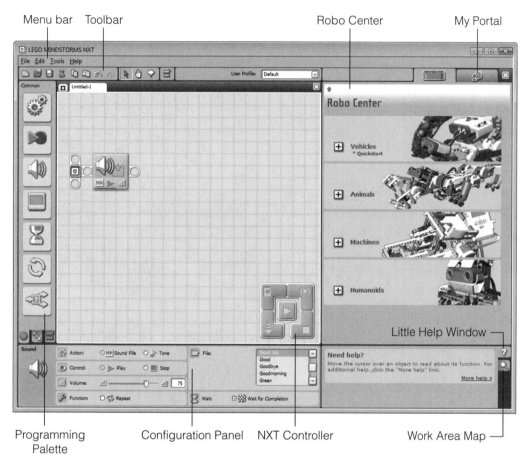

Programming   Configuration Panel   NXT Controller   Work Area Map
Palette

Figure 2.1
The Mindstorms NXT 2.0 Graphical User Interface consists of menu bar, toolbar, and a variety of windows.

let you define constants and create variables, which you will learn all about in Chapter 8, "Advanced Programming Techniques."

The Tools menu provides access to a collection of specialized windows, each of which is designed to perform a specific task. These windows include:

- **Calibrate Sensors**—Facilitates the re-calibration of sensors to tune their operations.

- **Update NXT Firmware**—Provides the ability to update the NXT Bricks firmware to the most current version, allowing you to take advantage of any improvements made by Lego.

Table 2.1 NXT 2.0 Keyboard Shortcuts

Shortcut	Windows	Mac OS X
Stop NXT	CTRL+B	Command-B
Copy	CTRL+C	Command-C
Download to NXT	CTRL+D	Command-D
NXT Window	CTRL+I	Command-I
New Program	CTRL+N	Command-N
Open	CTRL+O	Command-O
Print	CTRL+P	Command-P
Quit	CTRL+Q	Command-Q
Download and Run	CTRL+R	Command-R
Save	CTRL+S	Command-S
Paste	CTRL+V	Command-V
Close	CTRL+W	Command-W
Cut	CTRL+X	Command-X
Undo	CTRL+Z	Command-Z
Redo	CTRL+Shift+Z	Command-Shift-Z
Help	F1	F1
Displays the Common Palette	1	1
Displays the Complete Palette	2	2
Displays the Custom Palette	3	3

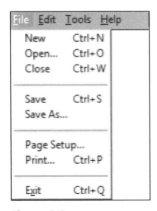

Figure 2.2
The Lego Mindstorms NXT File menu provides access to commands that manage program files.

- **Create Pack and Go**—Creates a Pack and Go file facilitating the development functions like My Blocks, Display Blocks, and Sound Blocks with other NXT developers.

- **Block Import and Export Wizard**—Provides the ability to import new programming blocks and to export custom developed programming blocks.

- **Image Editor**—Provides the ability to create and edit graphic and text files, which can then be downloaded and displayed on the NXT Brick's LCD.

- **Remote Control**—Provides you with the ability to remotely control your robotic creations, controlling both speed and direction.

- **Sound Editor**—Provides the ability to create and edit sound files that can be downloaded and played by the NXT Brick.

The Help menu contains commands that provide access to all the online help resources listed below.

- Contents and Index
- Online Support
- Online Updates
- Register Product
- About LEGO MINDSTORMS NXT

Toolbar

The Mindstorms NXT 2.0 toolbar, shown in Figure 2.3, provides single click access to commonly used commands and windows. Using the toolbar you can create, open, and save program files. You can also cut, copy and paste, and work with various tools. Icons located on the right side of the toolbar provide access to the Robo Center and My Portal windows.

Programming Palette

The Programming palette contains a collection of programming blocks or icons that are used in the creation of NXT-G programs. The programming blocks are

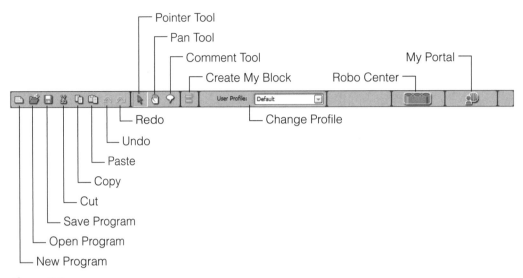

Figure 2.3
The Lego Mindstorms NXT toolbar provides access to commands that manage program files.

organized into three tabs, located in the bottom left corner of the Mindstorms NXT 2.0 GUI. These tabs are as follows:

- Common Palette—Contains the most commonly used programming blocks.

- Complete Palette—Provides access to all programming blocks.

- Custom Palette—Provides access to blocks that you create or upload into Mindstorms NXT 2.0.

Figure 2.4 shows the Complete palette. The Action block group is selected, revealing all of the programming blocks that it comprises. To use a block, click on it and then drag and drop it onto the Work Area.

Hint

You will learn all about Mindstorms NXT 2.0 programming blocks in Part III, "NXT-G Programming."

Configuration Panel

The Configuration Panel is displayed in the bottom left corner of the Mindstorms NXT 2.0 GUI whenever a programming block is added to or selected in

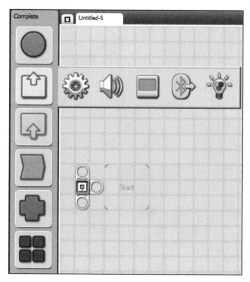

Figure 2.4
The Complete palette provides access to all of Mindstorms NXT 2.0's programming blocks.

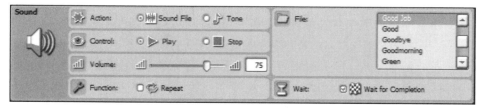

Figure 2.5
The Configuration Panel is automatically displayed whenever you add or select a programming block onto the Work Area.

the Work Area. The appearance and functionality of the Configuration Panel varies, based on the currently selected programming block. Figure 2.5 shows how the Configuration Panel looks when the Sound block is selected.

Using the Configuration Panel, you can customize the operation of the programming block, modifying both input and output and other attributes and actions.

NXT Controller

The NXT Controller provides you with the ability to communicate with the NXT Brick. It is used to transfer program and data files to your NXT Brick. It

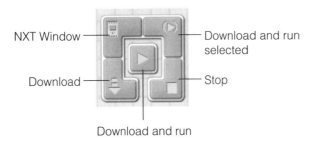

Figure 2.6
The second Time block has also been configured to delay program execution for five seconds.

also enables you to start and stop programs and to change NXT Brick settings. The NXT Controller consists of the following five button controls, shown in Figure 2.6.

- **NXT Window**—Displays the NXT Window, which is used to set up a connection to a NXT Brick, change its name, view battery, connection, storage, and firmware version and to manage NXT Brick memory usage.

- **Download and run selected**—Downloads and executes the selected portion of the current NXT-G program file to your NXT Brick.

- **Download and run**—Downloads the current NXT-G program file to your NXT Brick and executes it.

- **Download**—Downloads the current NXT-G program file to your NXT Brick.

- **Stop**—Halts the execution of the current NXT-G program.

My Portal

A big part of the philosophy behind Mindstorms NXT 2.0 is based on sharing and participating in the Lego Mindstorms community. The My Portal window, shown in Figure 2.7, provides a gateway to the http://www.mindstorms.com web site. The My Portal window shares space with the Robo Center. You also need Internet access to take advantage of this feature. To access it, you must click on the My Portal icon located on the left side of the Mindstorms NXT 2.0 toolbar.

You can use the My Portal window to access information on new models, program files, sound and image files, and wall papers. You can also use it to learn new tips and tricks.

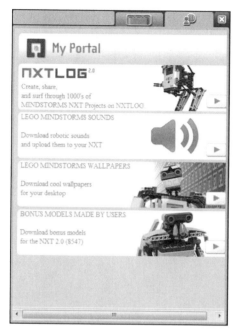

Figure 2.7
The My Portal window provides direct access to all kinds of resources that you can use in your robotic creations.

Robo Center

The Robot Center is located on the right side of the Mindstorms NXT 2.0 GUI. It shares space with the My Portal window. As shown in Figure 2.8, the Robo Center contains complete step-by-step instructions for creating four different robots. These projects are outlined below.

- **Vehicles**—Complete instructions for building the Shooterbot robot
- **Animals**—Complete instructions for building the Robogator robot
- **Machines**—Complete instructions for building a Color Sorter robot
- **Humanoids**—Complete instructions for building the Alpha Rex robot

Little Help Window

The Little Help window shares space with the Work Area Map and is located in the lower right side of Mindstorms NXT 2.0 GUI. The Little Help window is

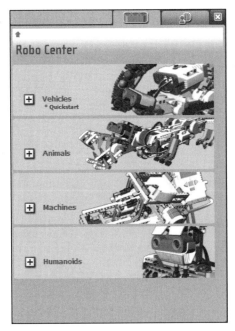

Figure 2.8
The Robo Center window provides you with access to building instructions for four different robots.

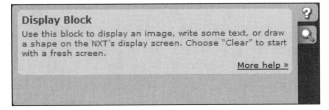

Figure 2.9
The Little Help window automatically displays help information based on the currently selected object.

displayed when the upper tab, identified by a question mark, is selected. To work with this window, shown in Figure 2.9, all you have to do is move the cursor over an object in the work area. In response, the Little Help window displays information about the object as well as a link to additional information. To see the additional information, click on the More Help >> link displayed at the bottom of the Little Help window.

When you click on the More Help >> link, Mindstorms NXT 2.0 displays the corresponding help file using your default web browser. For example, Figure 2.10

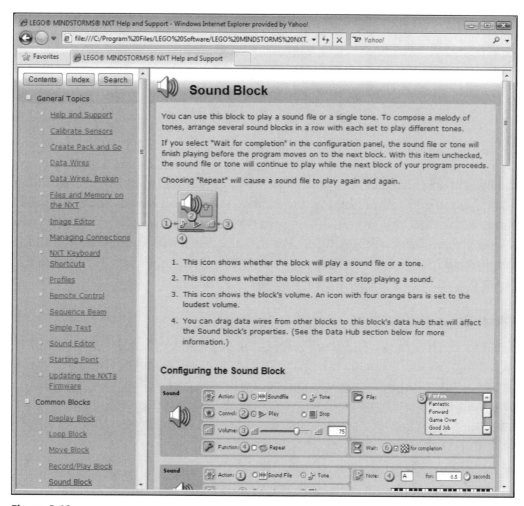

Figure 2.10
The help file for the Sound Block provides extensive information for that block.

shows the help information that is displayed if you click on the More Help >> link when the Sound block is selected.

The Work Area Map

As your NXT-G programs grow in size and complexity, they may become too large to be displayed all at once in the Work Area. To make navigation within the Work Area manageable, you can use the Work Area Map. The Work Area Map is in the same space as the Little Help window and is selected by clicking on

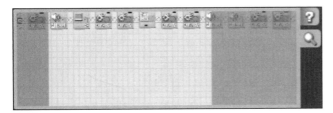

Figure 2.11
The Little Help window helps you to move around large program files quickly.

the Magnifying Glass icon. As demonstrated in Figure 2.11, the Work Area Map allows you to click and hold down the left mouse button on any area within the window and then move the cursor to a new area. As you do, the Work Area mirrors your actions, displaying whatever content is moved into focus within the Work Area Map. (The in focus position of the Work Area is identified within the Work Area Map by a white background.)

Work Area

The Work Area, shown in Figure 2.12, is the large gray gridded area located just to the right of the Programming palette. This area is boundless, meaning that it has no defined limits. It expands and contracts as necessary to allow for NXT-G programs of any size. The Work Area is tabbed, allowing you to create or open more than one NXT-G program at a time. To switch between programs all you have to do is click on their respective tabs.

As you will learn in later chapters, NXT-G programs are created by dragging and dropping different programming blocks onto the Work Area Map. As shown in Figure 2.12, every new NXT-G program starts out with a Starting Point sequence beam. To the right of the Starting Point is the word Start, enclosed within four small bracket markers, which identify where the program's first programming block must be placed.

Trick

You can make additional room available when developing NXT-G programs by temporarily hiding the Robo Center/My Portal windows. To do so, click on the orange Close button located on the far right side of the toolbar. This will remove the window that is visible, enlarging the amount of space allocated to the Work Area. To redisplay either of these two windows, all you have to do is click on its toolbar icon.

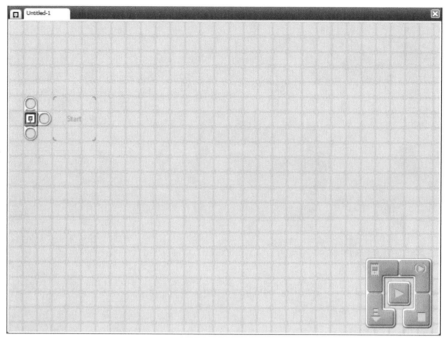

Figure 2.12
The Work Area is where you develop your NXT-G programs using Programming clocks.

OTHER NXT 2.0 GUI WINDOWS

The Tools menu provides access to a collection of specialized windows, each of which is designed to perform a specific task. Each of these windows and its purpose is examined in detail in the sections that follow.

Calibrate Sensors

The operation of your robotic creations can be affected by the conditions in which they operate. Specifically, changes in environmental lighting and sound may affect the way your robotic creations work. Because of this, your robotic creations may work differently when you move them from one location to another.

To manage the effects that different environmental conditions might have, you can calibrate the NXT sensors to specific environments, allowing your robotic creations to perform optionally in different environments. There are two ways of calibrating sensors. One is through the Calibrate sensor window, which is

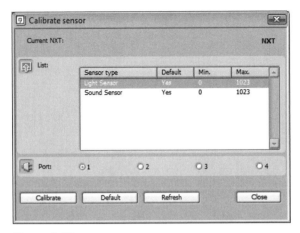

Figure 2.13
You can calibrate the sensors connected to your NXT Brick from this window.

accessed via the Tools menu. The other option is to use Calibration blocks within your NXT-G programs.

In order to calibrate sensors, you must connect your NXT Brick to your computer and turn it on. In addition, you must connect the appropriate sensor to the brick. Next, click on Tools > Calibrate sensors. The Calibrate sensor windows shown in Figure 2.13 will appear.

Hint

Neither the light nor the sound sensors are supplied with the Lego Mindstorms NXT 2.0 kit. These sensors can be purchased separately from http://shop.lego.com.

Trap

If the window is grayed out, make sure that your NXT Brick is powered on. In addition, make sure that it is connected to your computer.

Calibrating the Light Sensor

The following steps explain how to calibrate a light sensor.

1. Select the Light Sensor entry from the Listbox located in the List section.

2. Identify which port the sensor has been connected to on your NXT Brick by selecting the appropriate radio button in the Port section.

3. Click on the Calibrate button.

4. Look for the message Min Value: to appear on the NXT Brick's display, aim the light sensor toward a location that the sensors should measure as being dark, and press the NXT Brick's orange Enter button.

5. Next, look for the message Max Value: to appear on the NXT Brick's display, aim the light sensor toward a location that the sensors should measure as being very bright, and press the NXT Brick's orange Enter button.

At this point the NXT Brick and the light sensor have been calibrated to operate in the environment.

Calibrating the Sound Sensor

The following steps explain how to calibrate a sound sensor.

1. Select the Sound Sensor entry from the Listbox located in the List section.

2. Identify which port the sensor has been connected to on your NXT Brick by selecting the appropriate radio button in the Port section.

3. Click on the Calibrate button.

4. Look for the message Min Value: to appear on the NXT Brick's display, place the sound sensor in a quiet location within the environment that you are calibrating, and press the NXT Brick's orange Enter button.

5. Next, look for the message Select Max: to appear on the NXT Brick's display, place the light sensor within the environment that you are calibrating, make a loud noise, and press the NXT Brick's orange Enter button.

At this point the NXT Brick and the light sensor have been calibrated to operate in the environment.

Update NXT Firmware

Firmware is the software that is installed on your NXT Brick at the factory. It is responsible for starting the NXT Brick when powered on and for the NXT Brick's overall operation. From time to time, new versions of the firmware are

Figure 2.14
This window allows you to check for and apply firmware updates to your NXT Brick.

made available. These firmware updates may add new features and capabilities to your NXT Brick or may fix firmware bugs. To update the firmware on your NXT Brick, click on Tools > Update NXT Firmware. The Update NXT Firmware window appears as shown in Figure 2.14.

To determine if any firmware updates are available, click on the Check button. This will open your default Web browser and display a page on the Lego Mindstorms web site. Click on the Firmware link that is displayed on this page to view the most recent firmware update as demonstrated in Figure 2.15.

Click on the Downloads link to initiate the download of the most current firmware update. Next, click on the Download button that appears and save the download to your computer. Save the download file to one of the following locations.

Microsoft Windows:

```
C:\Program Files\LEGO Software\LEGO MINDSTORMS NXT\engine\Firmware
```

Figure 2.15
The Firmware page lists the current and most recent firmware updates that are available.

Mac OS X:

`Macintosh HD:Applications:LEGO MINDSTORMS NXT:engine:Firmware`

Once the download is complete, return to the Update NXT Firmware window and select the most recent firmware update from the Available Firmware Files: list. Then click on the Download button. You can track the progress of the download and installation of the firmware update by keeping an eye on the progress bars located at the bottom of the window. Once all three progress bars have turned green, the firmware upgrade process is complete. Click on the Close button.

Figure 2.16
Creating a Pack and Go function that you can share with other Lego Mindstorms developers.

Create Pack and Go

If you want, you can share any customized block's NXT functions, including My Blocks, Sounds blocks, or Display blocks, associated with the current NXT-G program with other Lego Mindstorms developers. To do so, click on Tools > Create Pack and Go. The Create Pack and Go window appears as shown in Figure 2.16. Next, enter a name for the function in the Pack and Go name: field. Click on the Browse button to specify the location where you want to save it. Click on OK to save the Pack and Go file.

Block Import and Export Wizard

If you purchase additional sensors for use in your robotic creations, you may find that you have to import new programming blocks into Lego Mindstorms NXT 2.0 before you can work with the sensors. Doing so is easy. Begin by clicking on Tools > Block Import and Export Wizard to display the Block Import and Export Wizard window as shown in Figure 2.17.

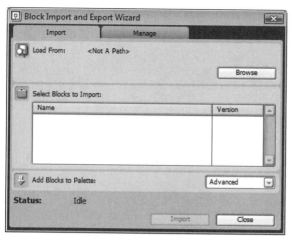

Figure 2.17
This window allows you to import third-party programming blocks.

Next, click on the Browse button and specify the location of the folder containing the new blocks. A list of available blocks should be displayed. Select the programming block(s) you want to import and click on the Import button.

Image Editor

Your NXT-G programs can display both text and graphics in the NXT Brick's LCD display. You can view and edit any of the graphic files that are supplied with the NXT software, or you can create your own graphics from scratch using the Image Editor, as demonstrated in Figure 2.18. The Image Editor works with any of the following graphic file types:

- .jpg
- .bmp
- .png
- .ric

To access the Image Editor window, click on Tools > Image Editor. To open an existing graphic, click on the Open button. To clear the drawing area, click on the Clear button. To create or edit a graphic, you can use any of the drawing

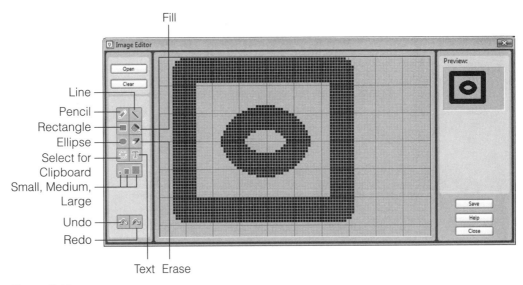

Figure 2.18
The Image Editor is used to develop graphics for display by your NXT-G applications.

tools displayed on the left side of the window. These tools work like their counterparts in any typical paint or drawing program.

The NXT Brick's LCD display is 100 pixels wide by 64 pixels tall. The grid system display on the Image Editor window is also 100 × 64. The preview pane on the right side of the window shows how the current graphic will appear when displayed in the NXT Brick's LCD window. Once you have finished creating or modifying a graphic, you can save your work by clicking the Save button.

Trick

By default the NXT software saves graphics as .ric files. If you prefer, you can save graphics using a different file format; just specify a .png, .bmp, or .jpg file extension as part of the filename.

Remote Control

The Mindstorms NXT 2.0 GUI includes a built-in remote control feature that you can use to steer your robotic creation and perform one predetermined action. You can also set and change speed. Remote Control is accomplished from the Remote Control window, shown in Figure 2.19. To access this window, click on Tools > Remote Control.

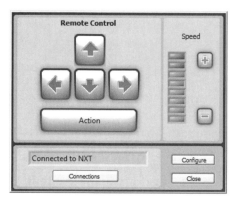

Figure 2.19
This window enables you to control your robotic creations remotely from your computer.

The Remote Control window is well suited to controlling robotic creations that use two server motors to control movement and the third server motor to perform an action. You can execute remote control in one of two ways. From the Remote Control window, you can:

- Click on the graphical arrow keys to set direction of the two servo motors used for movement.

- Click on the Action button to perform an action with the third servo motor.

- Click on the Plus and Minus button to increate or decrease the speed of the servo motors.

- Click on one of the eight speed indicator meter settings to adjust speed more than one level at a time.

Alternatively, when the Remote Control window is open, you can control your robotic creations using the keyboard shortcuts outlined in Table 2.2. The advantage of using the keyboard to remotely control your robotic creations is that with the keyboard you can push two buttons at the same time. As a result, you can execute gradual turns, giving you refined control over the movement of your robotic creations.

In order to control your robotic creation, you must establish a connection to its NXT Brick. This is done from the NXT window, which you can access by

Table 2.2 NXT 2.0 Keyboard Shortcuts

Shortcut	Description of Control
+	Increase speed
-	Decrease speed
A	Increase speed
Z	Decrease speed
1	Adjust speed to level 1
2	Adjust speed to level 2
3	Adjust speed to level 3
4	Adjust speed to level 4
5	Adjust speed to level 5
6	Adjust speed to level 6
7	Adjust speed to level 7
8	Adjust speed to level 8
Space Bar	Execute the Action server motor

clicking on the Connections button located at the bottom of the Motor Configuration window. Instruction on how to work with the NXT window is provided later in this chapter.

To assure that it works properly, you must configure how the Remote Control windows affect the operations of your robotic creation's servo motors. To set this up, click on the Configure button located in the bottom right corner of the Remote Control window. When you do so, the Remote Control window turns into the Motor Configuration window, as shown in Figure 2.20.

Begin by specifying which two of your robotic creation's servo motors are used for movement by clicking on the Move Motors: section's drop-down list and selecting the appropriate server motor pairing. The letters displayed in this list represent the ports to which the servo motors have been attached on the NXT Brick. Next, specify direction by clicking on the appropriate radio button in the Direction: section located under the Move Motors: section.

Next, configure the speed at which the robotic creation's third servo motor moves by dragging the slider control in the Action: section left or right to set speed to some point in the range of 0 (no movement) to 100 (maximum speed).

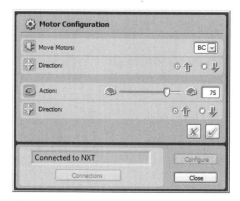

Figure 2.20
The Motor Configuration window allows you to configure and fine-tune the remote execution of servo motors.

Configure the direction at which the third servo motors moves by clicking on the appropriate radio button in the Direction: section located under the Action: section. When you're done, click on the checkmark button to save your configuration changes, or click on the X button to cancel your changes.

Sound Editor

You can enhance your NXT-G programs through the addition of sound effects that are played by the NXT Brick. Using the Sound Editor window, shown in Figure 2.21, you can record and create your own sound files or edit any of the sound files that come with the Mindstorms NXT 2.0 software.

Sound files played on the NXT Brick must be no more than five seconds long. The following procedure outlines the steps involved in creating or editing a sound file.

1. Click on Tools > Sound Editor. The Sound Editor window appears.

2. Click on the Open button to select an existing sound file, or click on the Record button to record a new sound file.

3. Although the Sound Editor can open or record audio files that are as long as 10 seconds, it can only save files that are no more than 5 seconds long. The wave graphic used to represent the sound file is displayed in

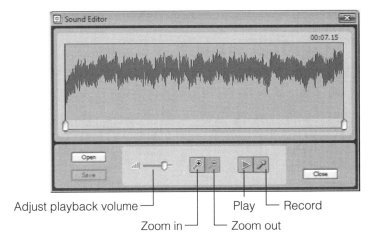

Adjust playback volume ⎯⎯⎯⎯⎯⎯⎯⎯⎯⎯⎯⎯⎯   Play   └ Record

Zoom in ⎯⎯⎯ └ Zoom out

Figure 2.21
The Sound Editor window lets you create and play sound files that can be incorporated into NXT-G programs.

red if the file is longer than 5 seconds. Wave files of less than 5 seconds in length are shown in green.

4. Click on the Save button to save a sound file that is less than 5 seconds long and specify a name for the file when prompted. If the sound file is greater than 5 seconds, use the two slider controls located at each end of the Sound Editor window to mark the beginning and end of a segment of the sound file. If the segment that is cropped is less than 5 seconds long, the wave graphic changes to green, signaling that it can be saved. Click on the Save button to save the cropped portion of the sound file and specify a name for the file when prompted.

If you want, you can also configure the value at which the NXT Brick will play the sound file by moving the Adjust playback volume slider left or right as desired. Any sound files that you create will automatically appear in the list of sound files available to your NXT-G programs.

Hint

Sound file volume can also be configured using the Sound programming block, overriding any settings you may specify in the Sound Editor.

MANAGING NXT BRICK COMMUNICATION AND MEMORY

In order to download the NXT-G programs that you develop on your computer into your NXT Brick, you must establish a connection with your computer. Connections are managed from the Communications tab on the NXT window. The window's Memory tab lets you see what is stored on your NXT Brick and provides you with the ability to manage its contents.

Managing Connections to NXT Bricks

The NXT window is shown in Figure 2.22. This window can be accessed by clicking on the NXT Controller's NXT window button or by pressing CTRL+I (Windows) or Command-I (Mac OS X). The NXT window can also be accessed by clicking on the Connections button located on the Remote Control window.

Any existing connections to NXT Bricks are displayed on the left side of this window. Detailed information about each connection includes the name assigned to the NXT Brick, the connection type (USB or Bluetooth), and the status of the connection. On the right side of the window you will see the name assigned to the NXT Brick, which you can change; you can also change its current battery strength, connection type, available storage, and firmware version.

You can refresh current connection information and initiate a scan for other NXT Brick connections by clicking on the Scan button. To establish a

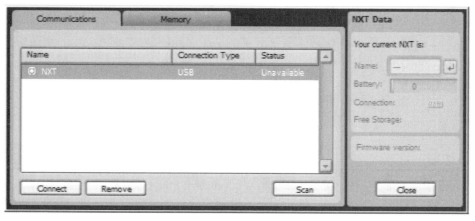

Figure 2.22
You can manage communication with NXT Bricks from the Communications tab.

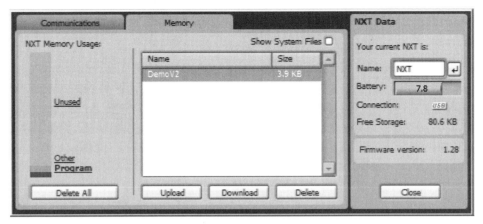

Figure 2.23
You can manage the files stored on your NXT Brick from the Memory tab.

connection to an available NXT Brick, select it from the list and click on the Connect button. To disconnect a connection, select it and click on the Remove button. Removed connections can always be added back later.

Managing NXT Brick Memory

The Memory tab of the NXT window, shown in Figure 2.23, provides a detailed view of the files stored on your NXT Brick. The NXT Memory Usage section provides a color-coded view of the different types of files stored on the NXT Brick. To view all of the files in a given category, click on the color for that category. A listing of those files is then displayed in the center of the window.

Using the button controls located at the bottom of this window, you can delete all of the files stored on the NXT Brick, upload new files from your computer, or download files to your computer. You can also select individual files stored on the NXT Brick. If you select the Show System Files checkbox, you can view and delete some or all of the system files that come pre-installed on the NXT Brick.

Hint

Removing all system files from your NXT Brick won't prevent it from operating. If necessary, you can reinstall these files by restoring your NXT Brick to its factory configuration, as described later in this chapter.

NXT Brick comes equipped with 130.8 KB of memory. However, much of this memory is used to store the NXT Brick's system software, which consists of things like example programs, graphic files, and sound files. As a result, you are left with somewhere around 55 KB of available memory to work with. As time passes and you download more and more NXT-G programs, graphic files, and sound files into your NXT Brick, memory can become scarce. From time to time you will need to remove files to make room for new files.

Restoring System Files by Reinstalling the Firmware

If you delete some or all of the NXT Brick's system files and find later that you need to restore those files, you can restore them. To do so, you must reinstall the NXT Brick's factory firmware. However, before doing so, make sure you back up any files on your NXT Brick that you want to save.

To reinstall your NXT Brick's original firmware, turn your NXT Brick on and place it face down. Next, using a toothpick or paperclip, depress the Reset button located inside the upper leftmost Technic hole (the hole that is immediately above the USB port).

Backing Up and Restoring Files

To avoid losing files that you delete from your NXT Brick, you can back up those files before removing them. To do so, select the file categories containing those files and then select the desired file and click on the Upload button. Later, if you wish, you can restore those files on your NXT Brick by returning to the Memory tab on the NXT window, clicking on the Download button, and selecting the files you want to download to your NXT Brick.

CREATING YOUR FIRST NXT PROGRAM

Now that you have reviewed Mindstorms NXT 2.0 GUI, let's dive right in and create your very first NXT program. The first step is to create and name a new NXT program. To do so, type Hello into the Create New Program field located at the bottom of the Mindstorms NXT 2.0 main screen, as shown in Figure 2.24.

When ready, click on the button labeled Go >> just to the right of the text field. In response, a new NXT-G program is created and displayed. Initially, the

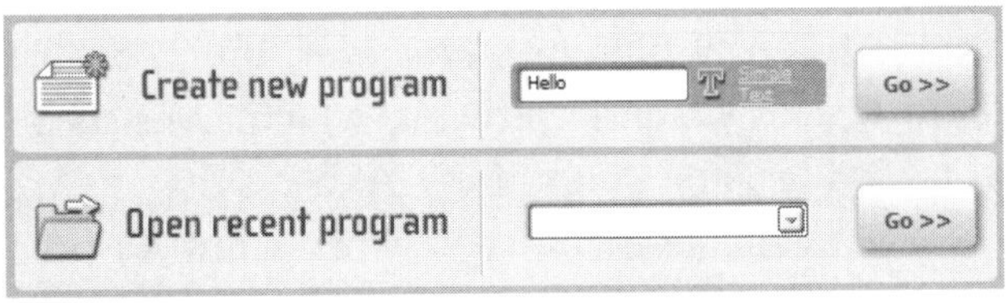

Figure 2.24
Assigning a name to a new NXT program.

program is empty. To add the programming logic needed to make your program work, you must add programming blocks to the program.

Begin by dragging and dropping an instance of the Display block from the Programming palette onto the Programming Area. This block provides the ability to display text or graphics within the NXT display window. When you release the Display block, it is automatically connected to the Start position. Your next step is to configure the Display block, instructing it to display a text string. To do so, select the Text option from the drop-down list located in the Configuration Panel and then type Hello World! in the Simple Text field, as shown in Figure 2.25.

Note that as you type in the text, a depiction of it is displayed to the right, showing how the text will appear once it is displayed in the NXT. Next, drag and drop a Time block from the Programming palette onto the Programming area. By default, it will automatically snap into place just to the right of the first block. Configure the Time block to pause execution for five seconds, as shown in Figure 2.26.

Next, let's modify the program to display a graphical smiley face. NXT-G provides you with access to different graphic files, all of which can be displayed on the NXT's LCD. To set this up, select the Image option from the drop-down list located in the Configuration Panel and then select Smile 01 from the list of graphic files shown at the bottom of the Configuration Panel. A depiction of the smiley face graphic is displayed in the preview window to the right, showing you how it will appear when displayed by the NXT Brick, as demonstrated in Figure 2.27.

To finish off the program, you need to add a second Time block. Drag and drop a Time block from the Programming palette onto the Programming area. It

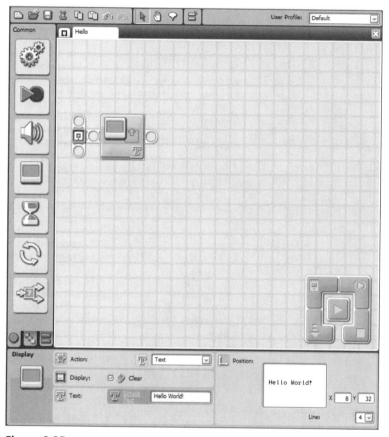

Figure 2.25
A graphic T character is displayed in the lower right corner of the Display block indicating its content.

should automatically snap into place just to the right of the third block. Configure the Time block to pause execution for five seconds, as shown in Figure 2.28.

At this point your new NXT-G program is complete. In order to test it, you must establish a connection to your NXT, download, and then run it.

CONNECTING YOUR NXT TO YOUR COMPUTER

The Lego Mindstorms NXT 2.0 kit comes with a USB cable, which can be used to establish a connection to your computer. To use it to establish a connection, power on your NXT and then use the cable to attach your NXT to your

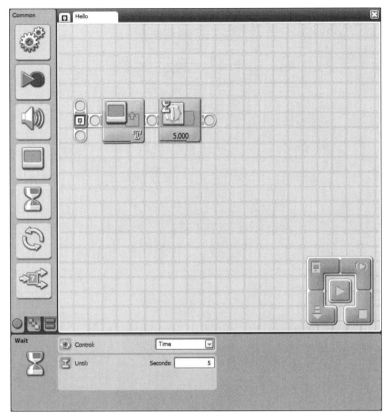

Figure 2.26
The Time block has been configured to delay program execution for five seconds.

computer. To turn on the NXT Brick, press its (orange) Enter button. In response, the NXT Brick powers on, displaying the Lego logo. This is followed by the display of the Mindstorms icon and the playing of a sound that signals that the NXT Brick has finished powering up. The main menu is then displayed.

In a few moments, your computer should recognize and install your NXT, displaying a message telling you that new hardware is ready for use. At this point you should be ready to download your new program into your NXT Brick.

Trick

If your computer supports Bluetooth, you can use it in place of the USB cable to connect to your NXT Brick. Instructions for doing so are provided in the Lego Mindstorms User Guide that comes with the Lego Mindstorms NXT 2.0 kit.

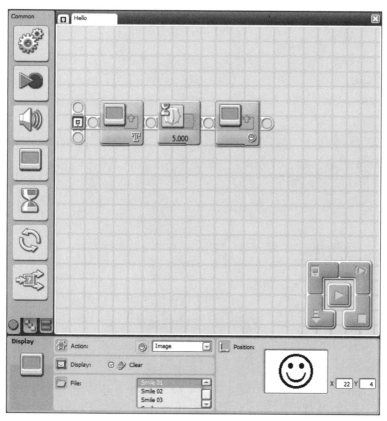

Figure 2.27
The program is currently configured to display a text message, pause five seconds, and then display a smiley face.

DOWNLOADING YOUR NXT-G PROGRAM

The NXT-G GUI provides you with a five-button graphical controller, located in the lower right corner of the Programming Area, for communicating with your NXT Brick. To download your program, click on the Download button. As soon as you click on the Download button, a window similar to the one shown in Figure 2.29 appears.

Once the program is completely downloaded, the window shown in Figure 2.29 disappears and your NXT Brick beeps, signaling the end of the process. At this point, you can unplug the NXT Brick's USB from your computer.

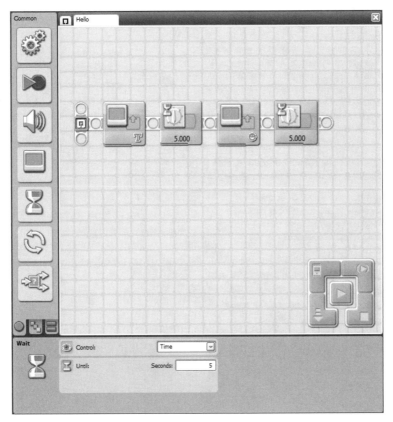

Figure 2.28
The second Time block has also been configured to delay program execution for five seconds.

Hint

If you run into any problems with the download process, make sure your NXT Brick has not automatically powered itself off. If it has, turn it back on and try again. If that does not fix things, double-check its connection and make sure that the USB cable has not become disconnected from your computer or NXT Brick.

RUNNING YOUR PROGRAM

Once your NXT-G program has been downloaded, it can be run. Just press the NXT Brick's orange button four times, and the NXT Brick will run the program. The precise series of events that occur when you do this is outlined below.

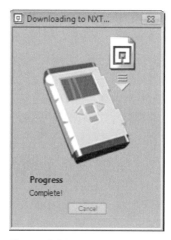

Figure 2.29
Status information is updated as the download process occurs.

1. Pressing the orange button the first time opens the My Files folder, which is the default item on the NXT Brick's main menu.

2. Pressing the orange button a second time selects the Software Files option.

3. Pressing the orange button a third time, by default, selects the most recently downloaded program.

4. Pressing the orange button a fourth time executes the selected program.

SUMMARY

This chapter provided you with a detailed review of the menus, toolbar, and windows that make up the Mindstorms NXT 2.0 GUI. You learned how to calibrate sensors, update your NXT Brick's firmware, work with the Image Editor and Sound Editor, remotely control your robotic creations, manage connections to the NXT Brick, and manage the NXT Brick's memory. Finally, you learned how to create your first NXT program, connect your NXT Brick to your computer, download your NXT-G program into your NXT Brick, and execute the NXT-G program.

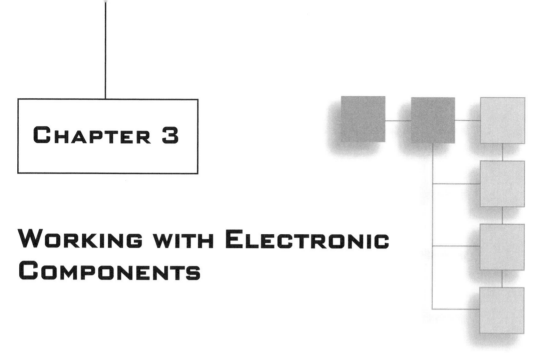

CHAPTER 3

WORKING WITH ELECTRONIC COMPONENTS

The Lego Mindstorms NXT 2.0 kit comes with 619 different pieces and parts. Of these, the NXT Brick and the servo motors and sensors represent the critical components in any robotic creation. Therefore, it is important that you have a good understanding of each of these components and how to work with them. In this chapter you will learn about each of the electronic components supplied in the Lego Mindstorms NXT 2.0 kit, and you will learn about their uses and capabilities.

The major topics covered in this chapter include:

- A detailed examination of the features of the NXT Brick
- A review of the NXT Brick's menu system
- A detailed examination of each of the sensors
- A detailed examination of the features and capabilities of the servo motors
- An examination of the cables used to connect the NXT Brick to sensors and motors

THE NXT BRICK

The NXT Brick is a programmable microcomputer. It is the computer brain that drives your robotic creations, executing programs you write and bringing them to life, allowing them to move and interact with their environment. According to

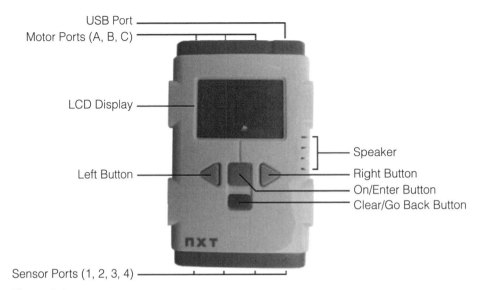

Figure 3.1
The NXT Brick is the brain of your robotic creations.

the Lego Mindstorms User Guide, the NXT Brick is an "intelligent computer-controlled Lego brick." As shown in Figure 3.1, the front of the brick is off-white in color and its top, bottom, and back sides are gray.

As shown in Figure 3.1, the NXT Brick has numerous connection ports, buttons, an LCD, and a speaker.

Hint

If you prefer a different color scheme, you may want to purchase the black version of NXT Brick. As of the writing of this book, Lego had released a special 10th anniversary edition of the NXT Brick dubbed the Black NXT Limited Edition (see Figure 3.2). This item was not yet available in the United States. When it is, you will be able to purchase it at http://shop.lego.com. There is no word on how long the black version will remain available. However, thanks to eBay and other similar venues, you should be able to find one if you are really interested.

The NXT Brick is powered by six AA batteries that go in the back of the NXT Brick and provide it with power, which is, in turn, also used to power the motors and sensors. If you prefer, you can purchase the rechargeable lithium battery pack shown in Figure 3.3 by visiting http://www.shop.LEGO.com and doing a

Figure 3.2
The black version of the NXT Brick.

search on Rechargeable Battery. As of the writing of this book, this part sold for
$54.99.

Hint

The NXT Brick is a remarkably reliable computer. However, like all computers, the NXT Brick may
experience occasional problems. If it becomes unresponsive, check its battery level indicator,
located in the upper right corner of the NXT Brick's display, to ensure that it does not need new
batteries. If your NXT Brick simply stops executing and does not respond to your commands, it may
be frozen. If this occurs, look at the upper right corner of the NXT Brick's display, just to the left of
the battery icon, to see if the NXT icon is spinning. If it is not, you will have to reset the NXT Brick,
as explained in Chapter 2, "Getting Started."

Figure 3.3
Over time the lithium rechargeable battery pack can save you money.

Technical Specifications

A breakdown of the technical specifications of the NXT Brick is provided in the following list:

- 32-bit ARM7 Microcomputer
- 256 KB Flash, 64 KB RAM
- 8-bit AVR Microcontroller
- 4 KB Flash, 512 bytes of RAM
- Bluetooth Wireless (Class II V2.0)
- USB port (12 MB)
- 4 Input Ports

- 3 Output Ports
- 100 × 64-pixel LCD
- Speaker—8 kHz Sound Quality
- Power: 6 AA Batteries

As you can see, the NXT Brick lacks the processing power of a typical desktop computer. However, it is perfectly suited to what it has been designed to do: provide intelligence and control over robotic creations.

Primary Features

The NXT Brick is packed with an assortment of features and controls, including:

- **Three output ports and a USB port.** Provide connections to servo motors and to your computer.
- **Four input ports.** Provide connections to the sensors.
- **A speaker.** Plays sound files.
- **Four NXT button controls.** Used to interact with the NXT Brick menu system.
- **An LCD display window.** Displays text and graphics.

These features and controls are explained more fully in the sections that follow.

Output/USB Ports

As shown in Figure 3.4, there are three motor ports located at the top of the NXT Brick. Using the cables that are supplied in the Lego Mindstorms NXT 2.0 kit, you connect the kit's servo motors to these ports, which are labeled A, B, and C.

Next to the three motor ports is a USB port, which is used to establish a USB connection between the NXT Brick and your computer using the USB cable included with the Lego Mindstorms NXT 2.0 kit. Alternatively, you can use the NXT Brick's built-in Bluetooth capability to wirelessly connect to your computer. To use Bluetooth, your computer must have either built-in Bluetooth or a Bluetooth adapter. For a list of compatible Bluetooth adapters, go to http://www.mindstorms.com/Bluetooth. You can also purchase the Bluetooth adapter shown

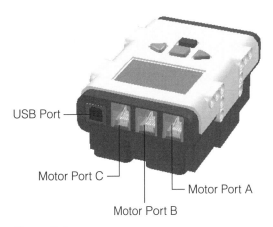

USB Port

Motor Port C

Motor Port A

Motor Port B

Figure 3.4
There are three connectors for servo motors and a USB connection at the top of the NXT Brick.

in Figure 3.5 at the Lego online store, currently for $37.99. To do so, go to http://www.lego.com and search on Bluetooth Part # 9847.

Input Ports

In addition to the motor ports and USB ports located at the top of the NXT Brick, there are also four sensor ports located at the bottom of the NXT Brick. As shown in Figure 3.6, these ports, labeled 1, 2, 3, and 4, are used to connect sensors to the NXT Brick.

Although you can connect any sensor to any sensor port when building your robotic creations, the Try Me programs that you can use to experiment with and text sensors require that the sensors be connected to their default ports. Table 3.1 lists the NXT Brick's default sensor port assignments.

Speaker

The NXT Brick has a built-in speaker through which it can communicate by playing different sounds through four small slits located on the right side of the NXT Brick.

NXT Button Controls

As shown in Figure 3.1, the NXT Brick has four button controls, which are used to navigate the NXT Brick's menu system and to issue commands. These buttons and their functions are listed here.

Figure 3.5
Bluetooth capability enables wireless communication between your computer and the NXT Brick.

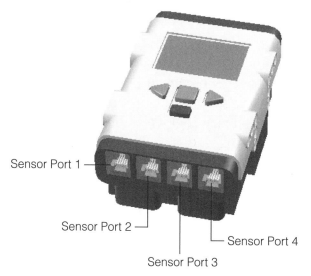

Figure 3.6
These ports are used to connect sensors to the NXT Brick.

Table 3.1 NXT Brick Default Sensor Ports

Port No.	Default Sensor
1	Touch
2	Touch
3	Color
4	Ultrasonic

- **On/Enter button.** This orange-colored button is used to power on the Brick, run programs, and select screen options.

- **Left and Right Arrow buttons.** These light gray-colored buttons are used to move left and right through NXT Brick menus.

- **Clear/Go Back button.** This dark gray-colored button is used to go backward in the menu system.

In addition to facilitating interaction with the NXT Brick's menu system, you can use the On/Enter and Left and Right Arrow buttons as sensors in your robotic creations.

LCD Display Window

As shown in Figure 3.1, the NXT Brick has a liquid crystal display, or LCD, through which it displays text and graphics. The monochrome display is 100 pixels wide by 64 pixels high. The LCD serves multiple purposes. It can be used to control the execution of robotic creations. It can be used to create new programs. It can even be used to display and play computer games, such as Tic-Tac-Toe and Hangman.

Figure 3.7 shows a depiction of the NXT Brick's LCD. When not running a program, it displays the NXT Brick's menu systems, which consist of a hierarchical collection of graphics menu icons. As shown in Figure 3.7, the LCD is large enough to display three menu icons at a time.

As shown in Figure 3.7, a series of graphic icons and text is displayed across the top of the display area. The first icon shows the NXT Brick's current Bluetooth

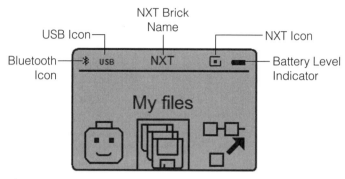

Figure 3.7
The NXT Brick's LCD display is able to display three menu options at a time.

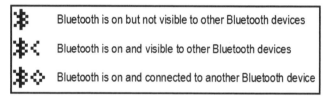

Figure 3.8
The NXT Brick indicates its Bluetooth status by way of a Bluetooth icon.

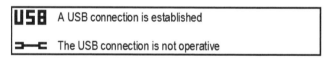

Figure 3.9
The NXT Brick indicates its USB status by way of a USB icon.

status. There are three possible states, each of which is represented by a different icon. Figure 3.8 identifies these states and their associated icons.

The second icon at the top of the LCD shows the NXT Brick's current USB status. There are two possible states, each of which is represented by a different icon. Figure 3.9 shows these states and their associated icons.

The name assigned to the NXT Brick is displayed as a text string at the top center of the LCD display. The default name is NXT. As covered in Chapter 2, you can change your NXT Bricks from the NXT window.

The fourth icon displayed near the upper right corner of the LCD is the Mindstorms icon. When operating properly, this icon should continuously spin. If your NXT Brick becomes unresponsive, check on the status of this icon. If it has stopped spinning, your NXT Brick has frozen up. Try turning it off and on. If this does not get the NXT Brick working again, you may have to reset it as covered in Chapter 2.

The last of the icons displayed at the top of the NXT Brick's LCD is the Battery Level indicator icon, which graphically depicts the NXT Brick's current battery level.

THE NXT BRICK'S FILE SYSTEM

You can interact directly with the NXT Brick through its menu system. The menu system consists of seven primary menus, each of which provides access to a different category of options. As is demonstrated in Figure 3.7, the NXT Brick displays three menu items at a time, each of which appears as a graphic icon. You navigate between these menu icons using the Left and Right button controls. You can open a menu by selecting it and pressing the On/Enter button. You can go backward within the menu systems by pressing the Clear/Go Back button.

Figure 3.10 identifies the seven primary menus in the NXT Brick menu system and shows the submenu options that each provides access to.

The following list provides a brief description of the functionality provided by each of the seven primary menus.

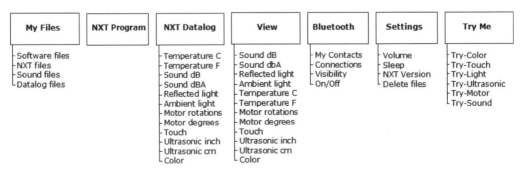

Figure 3.10
A depiction of the NXT Brick's file system.

- **My Files.** Provides access to the programs you have created.

- **NXT Program.** Allows you to build small programs in five steps using commands available under this menu.

- **NXT Datalog.** Facilitates sensor data logging.

- **View.** Lets you observe the real-time collections of data from sensors and motors.

- **Bluetooth.** Configures and manages Bluetooth connections.

- **Settings.** Configures NXT Brick settings.

- **Try Me.** Provides access to programs designed to test sensors and motors.

A more detailed examination of each of the seven primary menu options and their submenu contents is provided in the sections that follow.

My Files

The My Files folder provides access to NXT-G programs that you create and download from your computer to programs that you create directly on the NXT Brick. The My Files menu provides access to four submenus, listed here.

- **Software files.** Stores all of the NXT-G programs that you download into the NXT Brick from your computer.

- **NXT files.** Stores any programs you create on the NXT Brick.

- **Sound files.** Stores all of the sound files that are pre-installed on the NXT Brick as well as any sound files that you add to your NXT-G programs.

- **Datalog files.** Stores log files containing variable and sensor values generated during program execution.

NXT Program

This menu contains options that guide you through the creation of small NXT-G programs. These programs are created in five steps, each of which consists of a different command. Programs created from this menu require that sensors and motors be connected to their default ports.

NXT Datalog

Data logging is the process of recording data over a period of time using sensors. Using the options provided on this menu, you can configure the NXT Brick along with its sensors to collect the following data.

- Temperature C
- Temperature F
- Sound dB
- Sound dBA
- Reflected light
- Ambient light
- Motor rotations
- Motor degrees
- Touch
- Ultrasonic inch
- Ultrasonic cm
- Color

View

Options on this menu allow you to view real-time data collection from sensors connected to you next. With the appropriate sensors and motors in place, you can view data for any of the following:

- Sound dB
- Sound dbA
- Reflected light
- Ambient light
- Temperature C
- Temperature F
- Motor rotations

- Motor degrees
- Touch
- Ultrasonic inch
- Ultrasonic cm
- Color

Bluetooth

This submenu is used to change Bluetooth options on the NXT Brick. It contains the following four submenus:

- **My Contacts.** Stores a list of trusted Bluetooth contacts.
- **Connections.** Displays a list of current Bluetooth connections.
- **Visibility.** Controls whether other Bluetooth devices can see your NXT Brick.
- **On/Off.** Enables and disables Bluetooth functionality.

This menu also contains a Search command that can be used to look for Bluetooth-enabled devices within range of the NXT Brick.

Settings

The Settings menu lets you modify any of the following NXT Brick configuration settings.

- **Volume.** Allows you to modify the audio level at which sounds are played.
- **Sleep.** Lets you specify how many minutes of inactivity must pass before the NXT Brick puts itself to sleep. Valid options are 2, 5, 10, 30, and 60 minutes, or Never.
- **NXT Version.** Display NXT version information.
- **Delete files.** Lets you delete all of the downloaded programs stored in any of the following subfolders: software files, NXT files, sound files, and datalog files.

Try Me

Provides access to six sample programs designed to test the operation of the NXT Brick's sensors and motors. These sample programs are listed here:

- Try-Color
- Try-Touch
- Try-Light
- Try-Ultrasonic
- Try-Motor
- Try-Sound

Executing these tests is easy. For example, to execute the Try-Touch program, use one of the NXT cables to connect the color sensor to port 1 on the NXT Brick and then turn on the NXT Brick and select Try Me > Try-Touch > Try-Touch Run. Next, press the orange-tipped cone at the touch sensor. In response, a graphical image of a face appears and says "whoops." Repeat this test as many times as you want and then terminate the Try-Color program by pressing the Clear/Go Back button.

Trap

In order for each of the six tests to work, you must connect the sensors to their default ports on the NXT Brick using the RJ12 cables provided as part of the Lego Mindstorms NXT 2.0 kit.

THE SENSORS

The Lego Mindstorms NXT 2.0 kit comes equipped with four sensors, listed here.

- Color Sensor
- Two Touch Sensors
- Ultrasonic Sensor

These sensors facilitate the building of robotic creations that can touch, detect color and light, and even detect other objects. Two commonly used sensors not found in the Lego Mindstorms NXT 2.0 kit are the light and sound sensors.

These two sensors were part of the Lego Mindstorms NXT 1.0 kit. Some of programs found on the NXT Brick's Try Me menu are designed to work with the light and sound sensors. You can purchase both of these sensors online at http://shop.lego.com.

Hint

Several other sensors are available. Some are made by Lego and some are made by third-party companies. All can be purchased online at the Lego store. These sensors include:

- Compass sensor

- Accelerometer sensor

- Infrared sensor

- Gyroscopic sensor

- Temperature sensor

In addition to these sensors, Lego Mindstorms NXT 2.0 is also capable of supporting sensors from the Lego RCX kit. These sensors include the rotation, light, touch, and temperature sensors. However, a converter cable, which you can purchase from http://shop.lego.com, is required.

Color Sensor

The color sensor, shown in Figure 3.11, enables your robotic sensor to detect different colors and light, providing your robotic creations with a form of vision. In addition, this sensor provides a third function in that it can also be used as a lamp to generate light. The color sensor can detect six different colors: red, green, blue, yellow, black, and white. The color sensor supports a light sensor

Figure 3.11
The Color sensor provides your robotic creations with a form of vision, allowing them to detect different colors and variations in light.

Figure 3.12
The Touch sensor can be used to create robots that are able to detect when they come into contact with other objects.

mode, enabling it to detect light intensity within a room. It can also measure the light intensity of colored surfaces. The sensor returns a value from 0 to 100, where 0 represents complete darkness and 100 represents the brightest level. In lamp mode the sensors can display red, green, or blue light.

Touch Sensors

The Lego Mindstorms NXT 2.0 kit comes with two touch sensors. A touch sensor, shown in Figure 3.12, provides your creations with a sense of touch, allowing them to feel and react to things around them. The touch sensors attach to your robotic creation via connectors located underneath the sensor. In addition, the sensor's orange tip has a crosshair hole that can be used to further customize the sensor.

The orange tip of the touch sensor registers contact with other objects. It functions as a push button, registering two different states, pressed or released. A value of 1 is generated when the orange tip is pressed and a value of 0 is generated when it is not being pressed. Any of the following events can trigger a touch sensor:

- The orange tip is pressed
- The orange tip is released
- The orange tip is pressed and then released

Figure 3.13
The Ultrasonic sensor can be used to detect objects and determine their distance.

Ultrasonic Sensor

While the color sensor provides your robotic creations with the ability to detect color and light, the ultrasonic sensor (shown in Figure 3.13) provides your creations with the ability to see objects and to determine their distance. Using this sensor, you can create robots that can avoid other objects as they move about or track and target objects that come into range.

The ultrasonic sensor is capable of measuring distances between itself and other objects. It can also detect movement. It detects objects and measures the distance between the sensor and the objects. In this way, it provides your creations with the ability to determine their location. The sensor can cover a maximum distance of 255 centimeters (100 inches) and with a precision level that is within +/− 3 centimeters (1.19 inches).

The Ultrasonic sensor operates on the same basic principle as sonar systems, as depicted in Figure 3.14. It sends out high frequency sound waves, which reflect off of objects in front of the sensor. The sensor keeps track of how long it takes for the sound waves to bounce off of an object and return, and then calculates distances based on the elapsed time.

Figure 3.14
A depiction of the ultrasonic sensor sonar-like operation.

Like all sonar base systems, the ultrasonic sensor is able to see solid objects easier than software objects, Similarly, larger objects are easier to detect than smaller objects.

Using NXT Brick Buttons as Sensors

Using the NXT Buttons programming block, you can create NXT-G programs that can use the NXT Brick's On/Enter button and the Left and Right Arrow buttons as touch sensors. This allows you in effect to turn your brick into a collection of touch sensors. You will learn how to program using NXT-G and to work with programming blocks later, in Chapters 6–8.

SERVO MOTORS

Mindstorms NXT 2.0 includes a set of three servo motors, shown in Figure 3.15, that provide the ability to make your creations move and grasp things. The servo motors have a number of connection points where they can be attached to your creations. Servo motors have built-in reduction gear assemblies that include optical rotary encoders that sense and track rotation.

Using its servo motors, your robotic creations can move, rotate, and grasp. Each servo motor includes an integrated tachometer. A tachometer is a rotation sensor that precisely controls the rotation of the motors. Servo motors transfer motion through a pair of circular orange wheels that can be connected to your robotic creations.

Figure 3.15
Servo motors provide your robotic creations with the ability to move.

Servo motor rotations are measured either by rotations or degrees. 360 degrees represent a complete rotation. Servo motors operate with a precision or +/− one degree. When working with code blocks, you can specify either the number of times a servo motor should rotate or the number of degrees by which it should rotate. In addition, you can also configure a motor to run continuously for a specified period of time.

CABLES

As shown in Figure 3.16, the Lego Mindstorms NXT 2.0 kit includes seven different cables of varying lengths. These cables are used to connect the sensors and servo motors to the NXT Brick. These cables contain six wires and have RJ12 connectors.

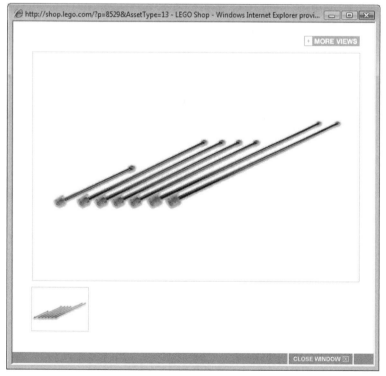

Figure 3.16
Additional sets of replacement cables can be purchased online from the Lego store.

Table 3.2 NXT RJ12 Cable Connectors

Count	Length
1	20 cm/8 inches
2	50 cm/20 inches
4	35 cm/14 inches

The only difference between the seven cables is their length. The Lego Mindstorms NXT 2.0 kit includes the list of cables outlined in Table 3.2.

Even though the cables that are supplied with the Lego Mindstorms NXT 2.0 kit look like telephone cables, they are not. Telephone cables are four-wire cables, whereas the cables supplied with the kit are six-wire and therefore not compatible.

Note

The cables are among the most delicate pieces in the kit. Their RJ12 connectors are easily broken if not handled carefully. Should one break, you can purchase replacement cables at the Lego store, located at http://shop.lego.com, as shown in Figure 3.16. At the time this book was written, a set of replacement connector cables cost $9.99.

SUMMARY

The electronic components supplied with the Lego Mindstorms NXT 2.0 kit are the key components in any robotic creations. Therefore, a good understanding of the components and how they work is essential to any Mindstorms developer. In this chapter you learned all about the NXT Brick, sensors, and the servo motors. You learned that the buttons on the NXT Brick can also be used as touch sensors. You learned about the NXT Brick's menu system. Lastly, this chapter provided you with an overview of the cables that are used to connect the NXT Brick to the sensors and motors.

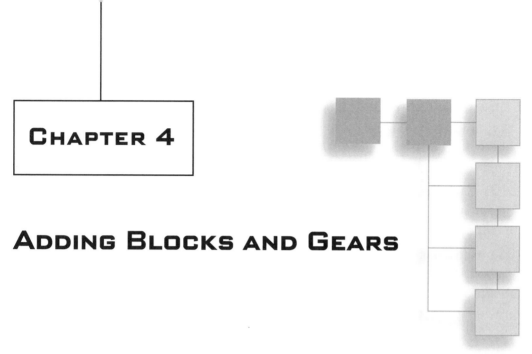

CHAPTER 4

ADDING BLOCKS AND GEARS

In Chapter 3, "Working with Electronic Components," you learned all about the NXT Brick and the electronic motors, sensors, and cables that are included as part of the Lego Mindstorms NXT 2.0 kit. These are important pieces, but they only represent 15 of the 619 pieces in the kit. A thorough understanding of the other pieces is essential to robotic development. In this chapter you will learn about all of these pieces, including how to identify them, their function, and their color and quantity.

The major topics covered in this chapter include:

- Beams
- Connectors
- Gears
- Other pieces

IDENTIFYING DIFFERENT PIECES AND PARTS

One of the challenges of working with the many pieces and parts provided in the Lego Mindstorms NXT 2.0 kit is that other than the NXT Brick and the electronic components, Lego has not assigned names to the other pieces. This can make identifying them challenging. As a result, different people refer to the same parts using different names. As you can imagine, this can lead to confusion. To facilitate part identification in this book, a number of different identification techniques will be applied to help simplify things. This will include using attributes like part length and color as well as categorizing parts into differently named categories and leveraging a few Lego terms.

BUILDING A FOUNDATION WITH BEAMS

One of the primary parts used in just about any robotic creation is the beam. Beams are used to build a sturdy framework. You can think of beams as being akin to the metal beams that are welded together to make up a bicycle frame. Without a strong frame, a bicycle won't support the rider's weight. The frame also provides the framework to which other pieces and parts are attached, providing the foundation upon which robotic creations are based.

The Lego Mindstorms NXT 2.0 kit provides several different types of beams. These include:

- Straight Beams
- Angular Beams
- T-beams

Straight Beams

Straight beams are one of the most commonly used pieces in any robotic creation. They have a smooth exterior, and their ends are rounded. Straight beams are perforated with circular holes that run down the middle of the beam. The circular holes are used to connect the straight beams to other pieces using other connector pieces. Figure 4.1 identifies the eight types of straight beams in the Lego Mindstorms NXT 2.0 kit.

Straight beams are identified by their length, which is measured using a unit of measure referred to as a *module*. A module is 8mm long, representing the distance between the outer edge of the beam and the center of the space located between its next two closest holes, which is the same as the distance between the center positions on either side of a hole, as depicted in Figure 4.2.

As demonstrated in Figure 4.1, this book identifies straight beams by specifying their length followed by their name. Straight beams come in three colors. The

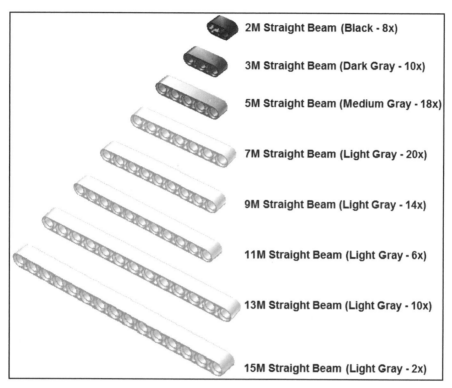

2M Straight Beam (Black - 8x)

3M Straight Beam (Dark Gray - 10x)

5M Straight Beam (Medium Gray - 18x)

7M Straight Beam (Light Gray - 20x)

9M Straight Beam (Light Gray - 14x)

11M Straight Beam (Light Gray - 6x)

13M Straight Beam (Light Gray - 10x)

15M Straight Beam (Light Gray - 2x)

Figure 4.1
Straight beams are used to provide robotic creations with a strong framework.

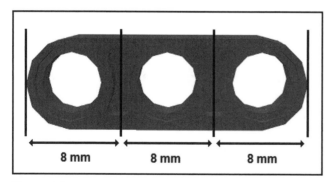

8 mm   8 mm   8 mm

Figure 4.2
An example of a straight beam that is three modules in length.

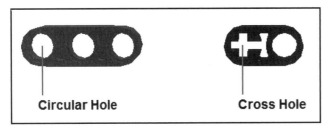

Figure 4.3
Except for the 2M beam, all straight beams have only circular holes.

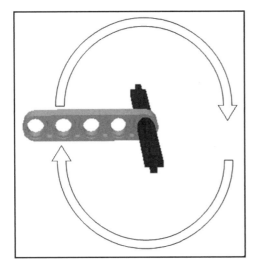

Figure 4.4
Circular holes allow axles free movement.

2M straight beam is black, the 3M straight beam is dark gray, and the 5M through 15M straight beams are all light-gray or white. However, because color is not an attribute that is needed to distinguish one straight beam from another, it is not included in the names of the beams referenced in this book.

With the exception of the 2M straight beam, all straight beams have circular holes at both ends. As shown in Figure 4.3, the 2M beam differs from other straight beams in that it has a circular hole at one end and a cross-hole at the other.

The key difference between circular holes and cross-holes is that when you place an axle in an open hole, the beam is able to spin freely as depicted in Figure 4.4.

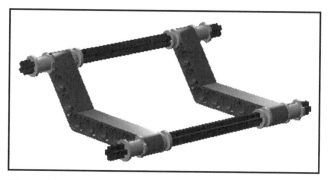

Figure 4.5
Using axles inserted into angle beam cross-holes in order to build rigid structures.

When an axle is inserted into the cross-hole of a 2M straight beam, a rigid connection is made and the beam in not able to move freely.

Both circular holes and cross-holes have their own unique purposes. Round holes allow flexibility and facilitate axle movement, which is needed in situations where the axle is connected to a gear or to a rim and tire. Cross-holes are useful in situations where you need to build strong rigid structures, such as the structure shown in Figure 4.5.

Angular Beams

Another type of beam included in the Lego Mindstorms NXT 2.0 kit is the *angular beam*. With angular beams, often referred to simply as angled beams, one or more sections of the beam are angled. Figure 4.6 shows all eight of the angular beams that are provided in the kit.

Angular beams can be used to create complex structures. They can also be used in all sorts of creative ways, such as to create claws for robotic cranes. Like straight beams, angular beams are measured and identified using modules. Angular beams range in size from 5M to 11.5M. Angular beams vary in their degree of angle, with the maximum angle of 90 degrees.

As demonstrated by the 9M angular beam shown in Figure 4.7, most angular beams begin and end with cross-holes, allowing for the creation of rigid connections using axles.

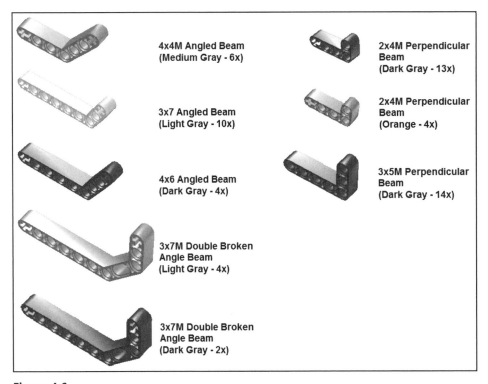

4x4M Angled Beam
(Medium Gray - 6x)

3x7 Angled Beam
(Light Gray - 10x)

4x6 Angled Beam
(Dark Gray - 4x)

3x7M Double Broken
Angle Beam
(Light Gray - 4x)

3x7M Double Broken
Angle Beam
(Dark Gray - 2x)

2x4M Perpendicular
Beam
(Dark Gray - 13x)

2x4M Perpendicular
Beam
(Orange - 4x)

3x5M Perpendicular
Beam
(Dark Gray - 14x)

Figure 4.6
Angular beams come in different sizes, shapes, and colors.

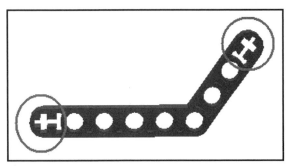

Figure 4.7
Most angular beams have cross-holes at both ends.

The T-Beam

The final type of beam included in the Lego Mindstorms NXT 2.0 kit is the *T-beam*. As shown in Figure 4.8, this beam is T-shaped and is 3M wide and 3M tall. This beam consists entirely of round holes. It can be used in various creative ways to connect pieces in ways that other beams cannot.

CONNECTORS

The largest category of pieces included in the Lego Mindstorms NXT 2.0 kit is composed of the connectors. It includes the subcategories listed here.

- Axles
- Bushings
- Pegs
- Angle connectors
- Steering links
- Cross blocks
- Peg blocks
- Other connectors

These different types of connectors facilitate connections, allowing you to connect and tie together different Mindstorms pieces into a cohesive whole.

Axles

Axles are cross-shaped shafts of varying lengths that can be used to connect to any Mindstorms piece that has a cross-hole connection. Axles are often used in conjunction with gears and servo motors to transmit motion. The Lego

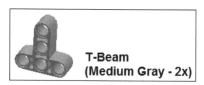

T-Beam
(Medium Gray - 2x)

Figure 4.8
Both sides of the T-beam are the same length.

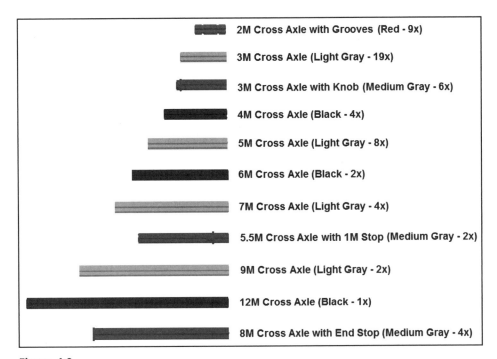

Figure 4.9
Axles are used to establish connections and to transmit motion.

Mindstorms NXT 2.0 kit includes a total of 61 of these pieces as shown in Figure 4.9. Axles can be used in conjunction with cross-holes on beams to create rigid connections and used with circular holes that allow the axles to spin.

Like beams, the length of axles is measured in terms of modules. Figure 4.9 identifies the length of every axle included in the Lego Mindstorms NXT 2.0 kit.

Bushings

One of the issues of working with axles is that they tend to slip out of their connections to other pieces. To address this issue, the Lego Mindstorms NXT 2.0 kit includes three types of bushing connectors. Bushings hold their axle's position firmly, locking other pieces that may be connected to an axle in place. Figure 4.10 shows the three types of bushing connectors supplied in the kit.

Figure 4.11 demonstrates the use of the bushing and half-bushing connectors. The half-bushing connector firmly holds its position on the axle where it is

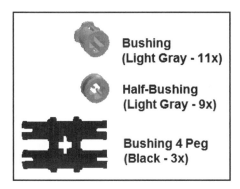

Figure 4.10
Bushings are used to establish rigid axle connections.

Figure 4.11
Bushings are used to cap the ends of axles, to hold pieces in place on an axle, or as separators.

placed. In Figure 4.11 the bushing has been placed at the end of the axle. Any number of other pieces can be placed between these two bushings, and their positions will be firmly maintained.

Bushings can also be used as separators in order to create space between different pieces attached to an axle. The Bushing 4 Peg piece has characteristics of both bushings and pegs, which are discussed in the next section.

Pegs

Though small in stature, pegs are big in terms of utility, providing you with the ability to connect beams and other types of pieces that have holes. As shown in

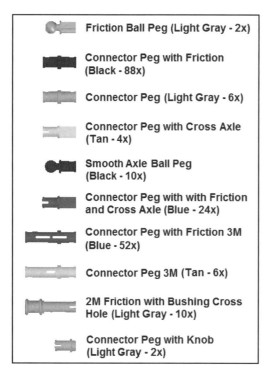

Friction Ball Peg (Light Gray - 2x)

Connector Peg with Friction
(Black - 88x)

Connector Peg (Light Gray - 6x)

Connector Peg with Cross Axle
(Tan - 4x)

Smooth Axle Ball Peg
(Black - 10x)

Connector Peg with with Friction
and Cross Axle (Blue - 24x)

Connector Peg with Friction 3M
(Blue - 52x)

Connector Peg 3M (Tan - 6x)

2M Friction with Bushing Cross
Hole (Light Gray - 10x)

Connector Peg with Knob
(Light Gray - 2x)

Figure 4.12
There are 10 different types of pegs.

Figure 4.12, the Lego Mindstorms NXT 2.0 kit contains 10 different types of pegs. In total, 204 of these pegs are supplied in the kit.

Some pegs are designed to fit circular holes, some are designed to fit cross-holes, and some are designed to fit both types of holes. In addition, pegs are either smooth or friction. Smooth pegs move freely within round holes, whereas friction pegs are designed to firmly hold their position. Regardless of the types of connections that pegs have, one feature common to all pegs is the *stop ridge*. As shown in Figure 4.13, the stop ridge determines how far the peg can get into a hole.

As demonstrated in Figure 4.14, pegs are used to connect different pieces together. In the case of Figure 4.14, two straight beams are ready to be connected using two connector pegs with friction.

Figure 4.15 shows the result of the previous example, once the two straight beams are connected by pegs. The result is a new sturdy connection.

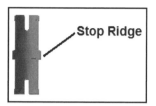

Figure 4.13
The stop ridge is a feature common to all pegs.

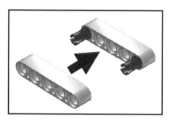

Figure 4.14
Creating a rigid connection using a pair of connector pegs with friction.

Figure 4.15
Two straight beams connected by a pair of pegs.

Angle Connectors

Another important category of connector is the angle connector, which is used to establish connections between axles. As shown in Figure 4.16, three different types of angle connectors are supplied with the Lego Mindstorms NXT 2.0 kit. Angle connectors can be used to connect two axles and to create 180-degree (straight) connections, to connect two perpendicular axles, and to establish 90-degree connections.

Figure 4.17 demonstrates the use of all three angle connectors. Here, two axles are connected using an Angle Connector 90-Degree connector. Each of the axles

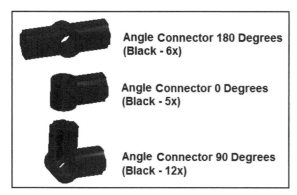

Figure 4.16
Angle connectors establish connections between axles.

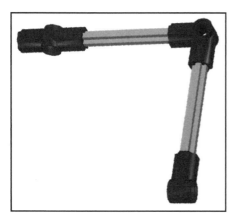

Figure 4.17
An example of the use of angle connectors.

is, in turn, connected to a different type of angle connector, allowing for additional connections.

Steering Link

The steering link, shown in Figure 4.18, is designed to establish connections with either the Friction Ball Peg or the Smooth Axle Ball Peg. These connections are very strong. They can be used to add a decorative look or to establish flexible connections in robotic creations that bend, stretch, and move.

Figure 4.18
The steering link creates sturdy connections.

Figure 4.19
The steering link connects to ball pegs.

Figure 4.19 shows an example of the steering link used to establish a connection between two Friction Ball Pegs.

Cross Blocks

Cross blocks, shown in Figure 4.20, are a combination of beams and bushings, providing a great deal of flexibility of use. Cross blocks combine circular and cross-hole connections. Cross blocks allow for the establishment of different types of connections. These blocks provide enough variety to tackle most every need and scenario.

Peg Blocks

Peg blocks are a highly specialized type of peg, combining features of beams and pegs. Peg blocks have circular holes, which run in multiple directions. Peg blocks facilitate parallel and perpendicular connections. The Lego Mindstorms NXT 2.0 kit contains three types of peg blocks, as shown in Figure 4.21.

Other Connectors

In addition to all of the different types of connections discussed so far, the Lego Mindstorms NXT 2.0 kit contains three additional connectors that do not fit into any of the previously discussed categories. These three connectors are shown in Figure 4.22.

Cross Block 3M
(Light Gray - 16x)

Cross Block Fork 2x2
(Light Gray - 8x)

Cross Block 2x1
(Light Gray - 4x)

Cross Block 90 Degree
(Light Gray - 8x)

Double Cross Block
(Black - 5x)

Cross Block 2x3
(Black - 6x)

Figure 4.20
Cross blocks combine qualities of beams and bushings.

The Cross Axle Extension is used to connect two axles, establishing a longer axle as a result, overcoming any axle length limitations in the kit. The Catch with Cross-hole connector connects axles that intersect perpendicularly. The Flexible Axle Damper 2M connector is used to connect axles that run in parallel and supports robotic creations that require flexibility.

GEARS

Gears are used to transmit motion. The Lego Mindstorms NXT 2.0 kit provides five different types of gears. As shown in Figure 4.23, a total of 11 gears is provided.

The first four gears shown in Figure 4.23 transmit motion through their teeth while rotating. Gears connect to one another, or mesh, by interlocking their

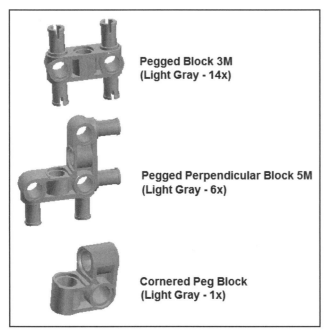

**Pegged Block 3M
(Light Gray - 14x)**

**Pegged Perpendicular Block 5M
(Light Gray - 6x)**

**Cornered Peg Block
(Light Gray - 1x)**

Figure 4.21
Peg blocks have features found in beams and pegs.

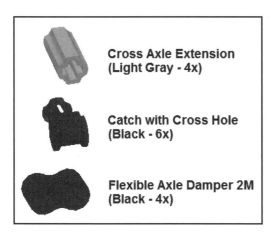

**Cross Axle Extension
(Light Gray - 4x)**

**Catch with Cross Hole
(Black - 6x)**

**Flexible Axle Damper 2M
(Black - 4x)**

Figure 4.22
All three of these blocks establish connections to axles.

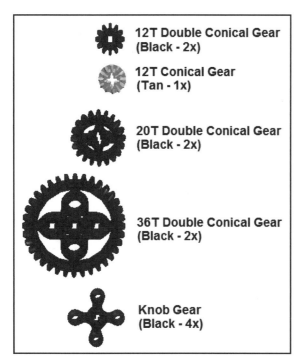

**12T Double Conical Gear
(Black - 2x)**

**12T Conical Gear
(Tan - 1x)**

**20T Double Conical Gear
(Black - 2x)**

**36T Double Conical Gear
(Black - 2x)**

**Knob Gear
(Black - 4x)**

Figure 4.23
Gears are used as a means of transferring motion.

teeth. The rotation of one gear results in the rotation of the gear with which it is meshed. Gears have cross-holes in their centers that are used to connect them to axles. The axles are, in turn, threaded through circular holes in beams and other pieces, allowing them to spin freely.

As shown in Figure 4.23, gears are identified based on the number of teeth they have. The first four types of gears shown in Figure 4.23 are conical gears. Their teeth, as shown in Figure 4.24, are shaped to allow them to mesh with one another when mounted on either a parallel axis or when mounted perpendicular to one another.

Creating Gear Trains

The use of two or more gears together creates a gear train. In the example shown in Figure 4.25, two 20T Double Conical Gears have been used to create a gear train using an angular beam. The gear train is pictured twice, providing you with both a frontal and a top view.

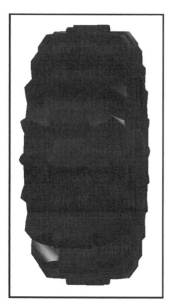

Figure 4.24
Conical gear teeth come to a single point on both ends.

Figure 4.25
A two-gear "gear train" mounted on an angular beam.

When used in pairs, each gear in a gear train moves in an opposite direction as depicted in Figure 4.26.

Gear trains can consist of any number of gears. In a gear train the gear that is responsible for transferring motion to the other gears is referred to as the *driver*

Figure 4.26
A depiction of the direction that gears move in a gear train made up of two gears.

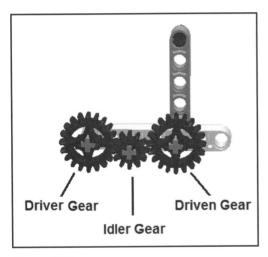

Figure 4.27
A hand crank made using a gear train with three gears.

gear. It is connected to a server motor via an axle. The last gear in the gear train is referred to as the *driven gear*. If there are any gears between the driver gear and the driven gear, these are referred to as *idler gears*. For example, Figure 4.27 shows a gear train made up of three gears.

Trap

As you add more gears to a gear train, more friction is introduced, reducing the overall effectiveness of the gear train. In principle, it is best to keep the number of gears in gear trains as small as possible.

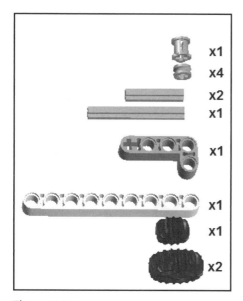

Figure 4.28
An inventory of the pieces needed to build your own hand crank.

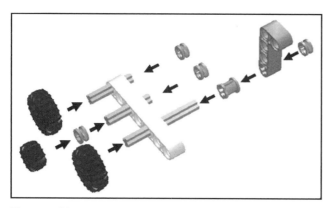

Figure 4.29
A visual depiction of the steps involved in assembling your own hand crank.

The parts needed to re-create the hand crank shown in Figure 4.27 are shown in Figure 4.28.

Assembly directions are provided in Figure 4.29.

Figure 4.30
You can use any number of idler gears in a gear train.

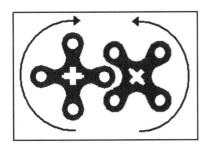

Figure 4.31
The knob gear only works with other knob gears.

Figure 4.30 depicts the direction that gears move in a gear train made up of three gears. As you can see, each gear moves in the opposite direction of the gear that drives it.

Idler gears are used to bridge gaps between driver and driven gears when they are too far apart to mesh. Idler gears can also be used to control the direction in which the driven gear rotates. Using an odd number of idler gears, you can create a gear train in which the driven gears move in the same direction as the driver gear. Using an even number of idler gears, on the other hand, causes the driven gear to rotate in the opposite direction from the driver gear.

The *knob gear* does not look like a typical gear. It has four circular knobs that rotate around its axis. The knobs mesh with knobs on other knob gears. Like other gears, it transfers motion from one axle to another, provided the other axle also has a knob gear. Figure 4.31 demonstrates how knob gears work together.

Note that knob gears rotate in opposite directions as they mesh together. Like other gears, you can create gear trains using knob gears.

Managing Gear Train Performance

Gear train performance is measured in terms of speed and torque as it affects the driven gear and the axle to which it is connected. Speed is a measurement of how fast the driven gear's axle is rotated. Torque, on the other hand, measures the strength at which the axle is turned.

You can affect speed and torque by controlling a gear train's gear ratio. Gear ratio describes the rotation of the driver gear relative to the driven gear. If, for example, a gear train's driver gear rotates three times for each rotation of the driven gear, its gear ratio is 1:3. Any idler gears in the gear train are ignored. An easy way of calculating the gear ratio is to compare the number of teeth in the driver and driven gears. For example, if the driver gear in a gear train is the 36T Double Conical Gear and the driven gear is also a 36T Double Conical Gear, its gear ratio is 1:1. If, on the other hand, the driven gear is the 12T Double Conical Gear, the gear ratio would be 12:36, which, when simplified, is 1:3. Thus, by changing gear sizes, you can directly affect gear ratio.

If you either decrease the size of the driver gear or increase the size of the driven gear, you are said to be *gearing down*. In a gear train where the ratio is 1:3, the driver gear must rotate three times in order to make the driven gear rotate one time. The larger the driver gear is in relation to the driven gear, the slower the speed of the gear train and the greater its torque.

If you either increase the size of the driver gear or decrease the size of the driven gear, you are said to be *gearing up*. When the driven gear is smaller than the driver gear, the speed of the gear train is higher and its torque is lower. As such, gearing up can be used to decrease the torque of a robotic creation and make it go faster.

Trick

An alternative to gearing down or gearing up is to programmatically control gear train speed using programming blocks, which can be used to execute greater control over gear ratio.

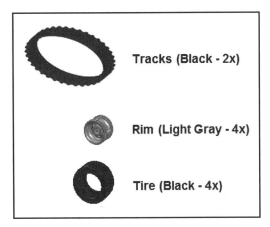

Figure 4.32
These parts are essential elements of mobile robotic creations.

Tracks, Rims, and Tires for Mobile Robots

Another important category of parts includes tracks, rims, and tires. These pieces, shown in Figure 4.32, are essential to any mobile robotic creation, providing them with the ability to move. The *rim* attaches directly to axles and transfers motion passed through axles to either tires or tracks.

Two rubber *tracks* are provided in the Lego Mindstorms NXT 2.0 kit and are perfect for making things like tanks, construction vehicles, and other such machines. When used, a track is wrapped around a pair of rims. When the rims turn, so does the track. In similar fashion, you can use *tires* in place of tracks to create cars and any other type of wheeled vehicle or machine. The tires are made to fit snuggly around the rims.

Other Parts

The remaining pieces and parts that make up the Lego Mindstorms NXT 2.0 kit are shown in Figure 4.33. The pieces shown on the left side of the figure are primarily decorative. The pieces shown on the right side of the figure have various purposes. The *magazine* is used to hold the kit's balls for using robots that shoot. The *shooter* provides a means of shooting balls. The kit includes a total of 12 balls, colored yellow, red, blue, and green. The *comb wheel* connects up to four axles. It can be used in various ways, as a stabilizer for axles or as an

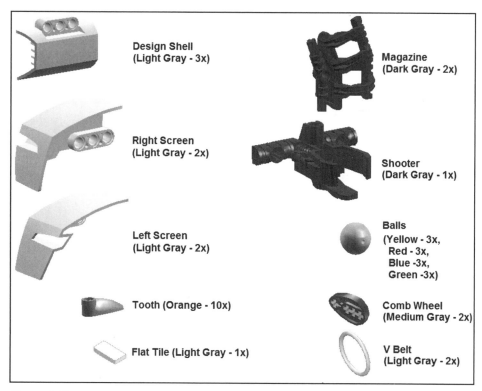

Figure 4.33
The Lego Mindstorms NXT 2.0 kit's remaining pieces and parts.

attachment that extends the effects of gears. The *V Belt* is a small rubber band that can be used to loosely bind pieces together.

SUMMARY

This chapter rounded out the book's review of the pieces and parts that make up the Lego Mindstorms NXT 2.0 kit. It focused on all the nonelectric and nonmechanical pieces and parts. This included learning about beams, connectors, pegs, and various other parts groupings. In addition, you learned how to work with gears and reviewed different configurations in which they might be used to transmit motion. This chapter also demonstrated the use of many of the pieces that were covered in order to further enhance your understanding of their usefulness.

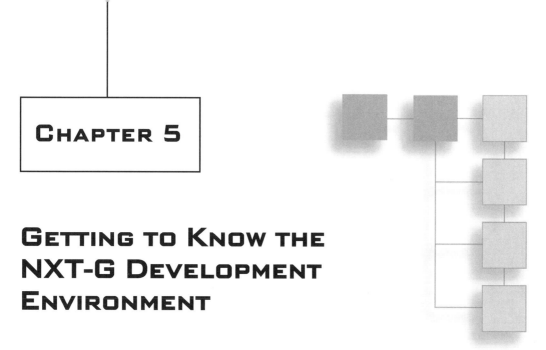

CHAPTER 5

GETTING TO KNOW THE NXT-G DEVELOPMENT ENVIRONMENT

Now that you know the basics of how to navigate around the Lego Mindstorms NXT 2.0 GUI and have a basic understanding of all the different pieces and parts supplied with the Lego Mindstorms NXT 2.0 kit, it is time to begin learning about NXT-G programming. Using NXT-G, you will write programs that control the operation of your robotic creations. NXT-G programs send instructions to the NXT Brick telling it how and when to operate attached servo motors and sensors. In this chapter you will learn a number of basic programming concepts and see how they apply to Lego Mindstorms NXT 2.0.

The major topics covered in this chapter include:

- Setting up personal profiles
- An overview of the program execution process
- An introduction to pseudocode and flowcharts
- Learning how to create new NXT-G programs
- Learning how to access programming blocks

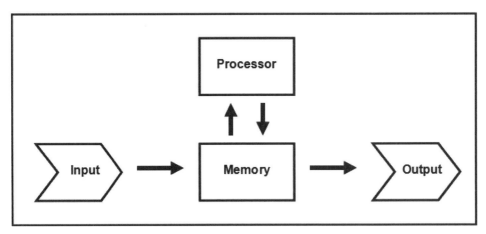

Figure 5.1
A depiction of the key components involved in program execution.

COMPUTER PROGRAM DEVELOPMENT AND EXECUTION

On their own, computers are not very smart. To do anything, they must be given very specific instructions. These instructions are provided in the form of computer programs. Figure 5.1 depicts the basic steps involved in the execution of a computer program.

Once a program is loaded into a computer's memory, the computer's processor processes the commands that make up the program. Programs process data passed to them as input and, in turn, generate output. In the case of NXT-G programs, input typically comes in the form of real-world data collected from sensors, and output is represented by the commands that NXT-G programs tell the NXT Brick to execute. This output might be commands telling the NXT Brick to engage its turbo motors, or it might be commands that tell the NXT Brick to play a sound file or display text or graphics on its LCD.

NXT-G differs from most other programming languages in that it does not support a text-based approach to program development. For example, the following statements are an excerpt taken from a Visual Basic application program.

```
//Excerpt from a Visual Basic application
If strCurrentAction = "FillCircle" Then
    Dim objCoordinates As Rectangle
        objCoordinates = _
    New Rectangle(Math.Min(objEnd.X, objStart.X), _
    Math.Min(objEnd.Y, objStart.Y), _
    Math.Abs(objEnd.X - objStart.X), _
    Math.Abs(objEnd.Y - objStart.Y))
    Pick_Color_And_Draw("FillCircle", objCoordinates)
End If
```

In text-based programming languages, program statements must follow a very specific set of syntax rules. Any failure to follow these rules results in syntax errors that cause programs to fail with errors. NXT-G, on the other hand, is a graphical programming language that makes use of graphical programming blocks, each representing a different task. NXT-G programs are built by dragging and dropping different combinations of programming blocks together on the work area as demonstrated in Figure 5.2.

By using programming blocks in place of complex program code statements, NXT-G simplifies program development while at the same time supporting the use of the very same programming logic and concepts implemented in traditional text-based programming languages. For example, NXT-G supports variables, conditional logic, and iterative programming logic. NXT-G also supports the manipulation of graphics and sound files.

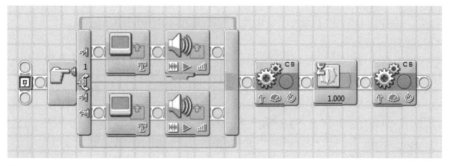

Figure 5.2
An example of how programming blocks are used in the creation of NXT-G programs.

Drafting Program Logic Using Pseudocode

Before you sit down at your computer to begin developing a NXT-G program for the purpose of bringing one of your robotic creations to life, you need to first know what you want to accomplish. A good way to get started is to outline your thoughts on paper, using regular old English as demonstrated in the following example.

```
If the user presses the sensor button
   Display a text message of "Alarm"
   Play the "Alarm" sound file
If the user does not press the sensor button
   Display a text message of "Try Again"
   Play the "Try Again" sound file
End
```

This high-level outline of the programming logic is an example of pseudocode. Pseudocode is an English-like outline of some or all of the logic involved in the development of a computer program. When initially outlining a program using pseudocode, your focus should be on the development of the high-level logic required to accomplish a given task. Don't worry at this point about specific programming blocks or their configuration. Once complete you can use your pseudocode as an outline when sitting down to write your NXT-G program.

In this particular pseudocode example, programming logic is outlined that would tell the NXT Brick what to do when it checks to see if a Touch Sensor has been pressed. The first line states the condition that is to be tested. If the condition proves true, the two lines that follow it are executed, displaying a text string and then playing a sound file. The fourth statement outlines the programming logic that is executed if the sensor has not been pressed. Here, a different text message is displayed and a different sound file is played.

Laying Out Program Logic Using Flowcharts

Another way of outlining the programming logic required to develop all or part of a NXT-G program is to use flowcharts. Figure 5.3 shows a flowchart that outlines the same logic that was presented in the previous pseudocode example.

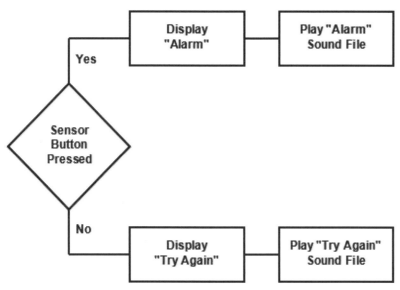

Figure 5.3
A depiction of the key logic needed to perform a particular task.

In this flowchart example, two separate courses of action are outlined. Which one is executed depends on whether a NXT Brick sensor button has been pressed. If the sensor button has been pressed, the actions outlined at the top of the flowchart are executed. Otherwise, the actions listed at the bottom of the flowchart are executed.

Once developed, you can translate the program logic outlined in a flowchart into NXT-G programming logic as demonstrated in Figure 5.4.

Here, a switch programming block is used to execute either of two sets of embedded programming blocks, depending on whether the NXT Brick's sensor

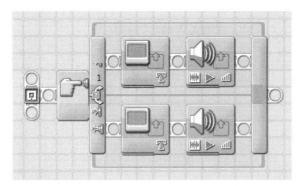

Figure 5.4
The implementation of the flowchart's logic in NXT-G.

button has been pressed. If you look closely at this example, you will see how clearly it reflects the programming logic that was outlined in the previous pseudocode and flowchart examples.

Turning Outlines into a Functioning NXT-G Program

NXT-G programs are created on your computer using the Lego Mindstorms NXT 2.0 GUI. Both Windows and Mac OS X are supported. Once you have created a NXT-G program, you must download it to your NXT Brick. Once downloaded into the NXT Brick memory, your program is converted into ARM, allowing the NXT Bricks 32-bit ARM7 microcontroller to execute it. This process is depicted in Figure 5.5.

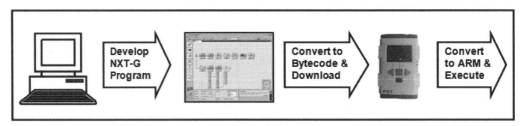

Figure 5.5
A depiction of the steps involved in creating and preparing a NXT-G program for execution.

Beginning a Program Development Session

NXT-G is a graphical programming language in which programs are constructed using programming blocks, which are dragged and dropped onto the work area and then configured to perform specific tasks. In order to access the work area, you must first open an existing NXT-G program or create a new NXT-G program.

To open an existing program, you must specify the name of the program by keying it into the Open recent program drop-down list or by selecting it from the drop-down list as shown in Figure 5.6 and then clicking on the associated Go>> button.

Figure 5.6
Opening an existing NXT-G program.

Figure 5.7
Naming a new NXT-G program.

Hint

You can also access program files for the currently selected profile by pressing Ctrl+O on Windows or Command-O on Mac OS X. In addition, you can select program files by clicking on File > Open.

To create a new NXT-G program, type a name for the program in the Create new program field as shown in Figure 5.7 and click on the associated Go>> button.

Hint

You can also create a new NXT-G program by pressing Ctrl+N on Windows or Command-N on Mac OS X. Alternatively, you can create a new program file by clicking on File > New.

The Lego Mindstorms NXT 2.0 GUI automatically assigns the default name Untitled-1 to your first new program. The number at the end of the new program name is automatically incremented with each new program you create after that. However, you can and should provide your NXT-G programs with unique names of your own choosing, preferably assigning names that help identify programs and describe their purpose.

Understanding Developer Profiles

The Lego Mindstorms NXT 2.0 GUI associates NXT-G program files with the developer profile that is used to create them. When installed, Lego Mindstorms NXT 2.0 automatically defines a single profile named Default. Unless new profiles are created, all NXT-G programs that are created are automatically associated with this profile, meaning that they are readily visible to each developer who works with the computer.

When more than one developer shares a single computer, it's a good practice to set up a unique profile for each developer. This way, each developer will only see the NXT-G programs that she has created. This helps prevent one developer from accidentally opening and modifying someone else's NXT-G program.

Hint

> In addition to keeping NXT-G programs separate, developer profiles also keep other program files separated, including things like sound and graphic files. Note, however, that developer profiles are not a security feature. There is nothing to prevent you from selecting someone else's profile.

Selecting a Developer Profile

To select your profile, all you have to do is click on the User Profile: drop-down list located on the Lego Mindstorms NXT 2.0 toolbar shown in Figure 5.8 and select it.

Figure 5.8
Selecting a developer profile.

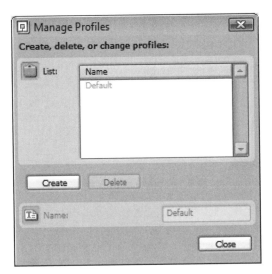

Figure 5.9
Managing developer profiles.

Creating a New Developer Profile

To create a new developer profile select Edit > Manage Profiles from the Lego Mindstorms NXT 2.0 toolbar. In response, the Manage Profiles dialog is displayed, as shown in Figure 5.9. From here you can create, delete, and rename developer profiles.

The following procedure outlines the steps involved in creating a new developer profile.

Step-by-Step

1. Click on the Create button. This adds a new profile with a default name of Profile_1 to the list of developer profiles and enables the Name: field.

2. Overtype the default profile name with a unique name of your own choosing, as demonstrated in Figure 5.10.

3. Press Enter to assign the new name to the profile.

4. Repeat the above steps to create as many profiles as needed and then click on the Close button when done.

Figure 5.10
Creating a new developer profile named Jerry Ford.

Hint

> You can rename developer profiles at any time from the Manage Profiles dialog box by selecting
> one and overtyping its name. You can delete them by selecting one or more from the list of profile
> names and then clicking the Delete button.

Giving Yourself More Room to Work

Once you have created or opened a NXT-G program, the Lego Mindstorms
NXT 2.0 GUI displays a new tab in the work area. This tab displays the name of
the NXT-G program you have opened or created. You can simultaneously open
or create and work with as many NXT-G programs as you wish and then switch
between them by clicking on their tab at the top of the work area.

As shown in Figure 5.11, the work area is a gridded window that displays the
Starting Point and the NXT Controller. The Starting Point identifies the location
where your NXT-G program's first programming block will go. The NXT
Controller is used to download and execute all or part of your NXT-G program
onto your NXT Brick.

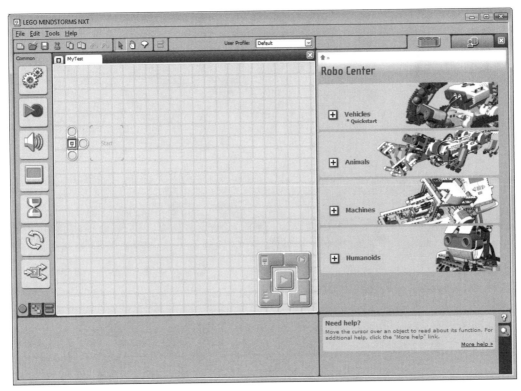

Figure 5.11
The work area is where you will develop the programming logic for your NXT-G programs.

By allowing you to switch between NXT-G programs by clicking on their tabs, the Lego Mindstorms NXT 2.0 GUI makes efficient use of work area space. The work area represents a boundless space with no height or width limits. As your NXT-G programs grow in size, they may exceed the viewable limits of the work area, in which case the GUI automatically shifts downward or to the right as needed to allow more room for programming blocks.

If you wish, you can increase the amount of visible space allocated to the work area by clicking on the orange Remove button located on the far right side of the GUI toolbar. This action hides the Robo Center, increasing the size of the work area, as demonstrated in Figure 5.12.

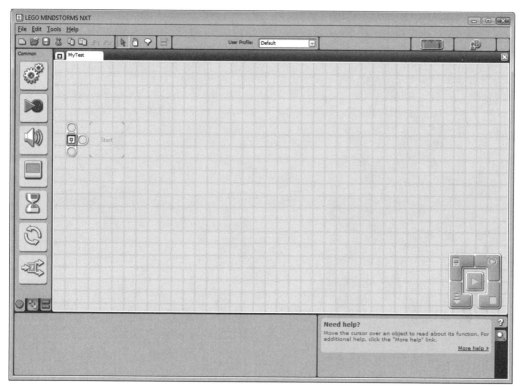

Figure 5.12
By closing the Robo Center you can increase your view of the work area.

You can restore the work area to its original size and redisplay the Robo Center at any time by clicking on the Robo Center Icon (an orange 3M beam) located on the GUI toolbar.

ACCESSING PROGRAMMING BLOCKS

NXT-G programs are made up of programming blocks. Each programming block represents a different type of action. Each programming block is configurable. Programming blocks have plain, easy to understand, English names and are used to formulate the programming logic in NXT-G programs. As shown in

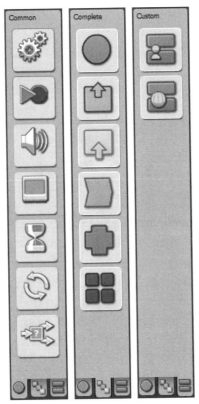

Figure 5.13
Programming blocks are accessed through one of three tabs on the Programming palette.

Figure 5.13, programming blocks are organized and presented on the three tabs that make up the Programming palette.

The Programming palette is located on the left side of the GUI and only one of its tabs is visible at a time. Programming blocks are added to the NXT-G program by dragging and dropping them onto the work area. After programming blocks are added to a NXT-G program, you can configure the manner in which each programming block executes by modifying parameters that are displayed in the Configuration Panel whenever a programming block is selected. Each programming block is unique and therefore has different parameters, specific to the tasks that the programming block performs.

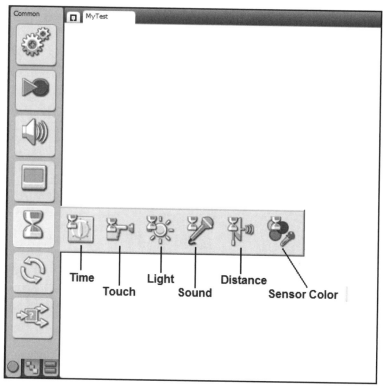

Figure 5.14
The most commonly accessed programming blocks are accessible from the Common tab.

Common Palette Programming Blocks

The programming blocks that you are likely to use most often are all located on the Programming palette's Common tab as shown in Figure 5.14.

As shown in Figure 5.15, there are seven programming blocks displayed on the Common palette. These blocks and their purpose are outlined in Table 5.1.

Each entry listed in Table 5.1 corresponds to an individual programming block except for the Wait entry. As shown in Figure 5.15, when you move the mouse pointer over the Wait programming block icon, the Programming palette expands to show the six most commonly used variations of this block: Time, Touch, Light, Sound, Distance, and Sensor Color. Other variations of the Wait

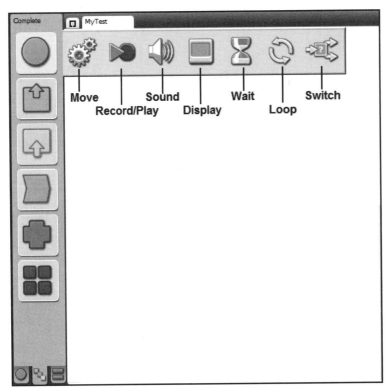

Figure 5.15
The Common group provides access to the same programming blocks found on the Common palette.

programming block are accessible when configuring the Wait programming block.

Complete Palette Programming Blocks

The Complete palette provides access to all programming blocks, even those displayed on the Common tab. In total, the Complete palette provides access to 39 programming blocks, organized into 6 categories. These categories are outlined in Table 5.2.

Common Programming Blocks

As shown in Figure 5.15, the Common group on the Complete palette contains a list of all of the blocks found on the Common palette.

Table 5.1 Common Programming Blocks

Icon	Name	Description
	Move	Moves a robotic creation forward or backward.
	Record/Play	Records an action manually performed with a robotic creation and then allows that action to be replayed.
	Sound	Instructs the NXT Brick to play a sound file.
	Display	Displays text, shapes, and images on the NXT Brick's LCD.
	Wait	Pauses program execution for a period of time.
	Loop	Repeats the execution of specified programming blocks.
	Switch	Choose between two alternate courses of actions based on a sensor or input value.

Table 5.2 Complete Palette Programming Block Groups

Icon	Name	Description
	Common	Contains a list of all of the blocks found on the Common tab.
	Action	Contains a list of blocks that send commands to the NXT Brick in order to execute specific actions.
	Sensor	Contains blocks that read sensors.
	Flow	Contains a list of blocks that can be used to alter the logical execution flow of a program.
	Data	Contains a list of blocks that define, generate, and process program data.
	Advanced	Performs miscellaneous functions not associated with other block groups.

Table 5.3 Common Programming Blocks

Icon	Name	Description
	Move	Moves a robotic creation forward or backward.
	Record/Play	Records an action manually performed with a robotic creation and then allows that action to be replayed.
	Sound	Instructs the NXT Brick to play sound files.
	Display	Displays text, shapes, and images on the NXT Brick's LCD.
	Wait	Pauses program execution for a period of time.
	Loop	Repeats the execution of specified programming blocks.
	Switch	Chooses between two alternate courses of action based on the analysis of sensor or input value.

These Common programming blocks are outlined in Table 5.3.

Action Programming Blocks

As shown in Figure 5.16, the Action group on the Complete palette contains a list of blocks that send commands to the NXT Blocks in order to execute specific actions.

These programming blocks are outlined in Table 5.4.

Sensor Programming Blocks

As shown in Figure 5.17, the Sensor Group on the Complete palette contains programming blocks that read sensor data from robotic sensors and pass data to other programming blocks through data wires.

Hint

Data wires are data pathways that you can draw between programming blocks in order to pass data from one programming block to another.

Figure 5.16
The Action group displays five programming blocks.

Table 5.4 Action Programming Blocks

Icon	Name	Description
	Motor	Provides precise control of a motor's speed.
	Sound	Plays a sound file or a tone.
	Display	Displays an image, text, or shape on the NXT Brick's LCD screen or clears the LCD screen.
	Send Message	This block is used to send a wireless message to your NXT Brick via a Bluetooth connection.
	Color Lamp	Controls the Color Sensor's lamp function, emitting red, green, or blue light.

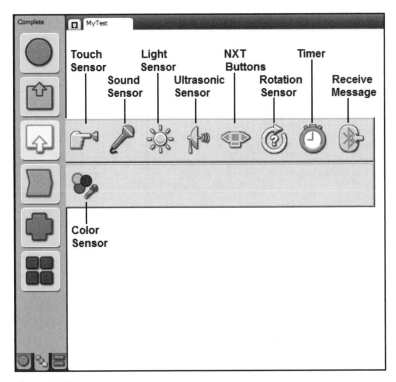

Figure 5.17
The Sensor group displays nine programming blocks.

There are a total of nine Sensor programming blocks, as outlined in Table 5.5.

Flow Programming Blocks

As shown in Figure 5.18, the Flow group on the Complete palette contains a list of blocks that can be used to alter the logical execution flow of a program.

There are a total of four Flow programming blocks, as outlined in Table 5.6.

Data Programming Blocks

As shown in Figure 5.19, the Data group on the Complete palette contains a list of blocks that define, generate, and process program data in a variety of different ways.

Table 5.5 Sensor Programming Blocks

Icon	Name	Description
	Touch Sensor	Sends a true/false signal through a data wire based on the current condition of a touch sensor.
	Sound Sensor	Detects sounds and reports on sound level.
	Light Sensor	Detects ambient light.
	Ultrasonic Sensor	Establishes a connection to another Bluetooth device.
	NXT Buttons	Sends true signal through a data wire whenever a NXT button is activated.
	Rotation Sensor	Counts the number of degrees or the number of rotations that a motor turns.
	Timer	This block reads the timer's current value or restarts the timer.
	Receive Message	Enables the receipt of wireless messages.
	Color Sensor	Enables the detection of different colors and the measurement of light intensity.

Data programming blocks also pass data to other programming blocks via data wires. There are a total of seven Data programming blocks, as outlined in Table 5.7.

Advanced Programming Blocks

As shown in Figure 5.20, the Advanced group on the Complete palette contains a list of blocks that perform functions not associated with other block groups.

There are a total of seven Advanced programming blocks, as outlined in Table 5.8.

Custom Palette Programming Blocks

The Custom tab displays programming blocks that you have custom created or that you have downloaded from the Internet. Custom blocks are visible only on the Custom palette. There are two categories of custom programming blocks, My blocks and Web blocks. To display your My blocks or Web blocks, simply

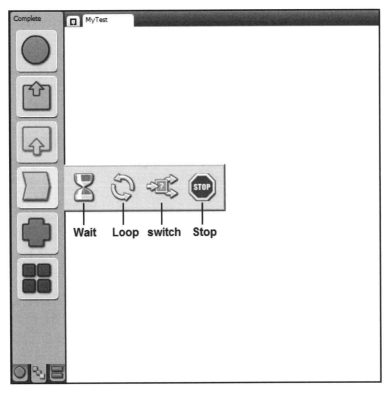

Figure 5.18
The Flow group contains four programming blocks.

Table 5.6 Flow Programming Blocks

Icon	Name	Description
⧗	Wait	Pauses NXT-G program execution.
↻	Loop	Repeats the execution of specified programming blocks.
⇥	Switch	Chooses between two alternate courses of action based on the analysis of sensor or input value.
🛑	Stop	Halts program execution and any running motors.

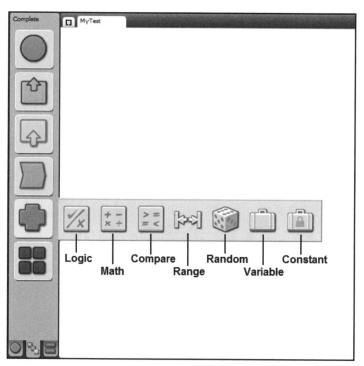

Figure 5.19
The Data group contains seven programming blocks.

Table 5.7 Data Programming Blocks

Icon	Name	Description
	Logic	Reviews inputs and returns a true/false value.
	Math	Performs arithmetic, subtraction, multiplication, and division operations.
	Compare	Determines if a number is greater than, less than, or equal to another number.
	Range	Determines whether a number is inside a range of numbers.
	Random	Generates a random number.
	Variable	Reads or writes variable values.
	Constant	Returns a value stored in a constant.

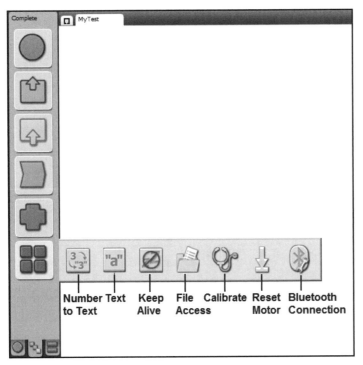

Figure 5.20
The Advanced group contains seven programming blocks.

Table 5.8 Advanced Programming Blocks

Icon	Name	Description
	Number to Text	Takes a number and turns it into a displayable text string.
	Text	Adds text strings together in order to create a longer text string.
	Keep Alive	Prevents the NXT Brick from going to sleep.
	File Access	Saves data to files on your NXT Brick.
	Calibrate	Calibrates the minimum and maximum values detected by sound/light sensors.
	Reset Motor	Disables the automatic error correction for servo motors.
	Bluetooth Connection	Establishes a connection to connect to another Bluetooth device or disables/enables Bluetooth functionality.

Table 5.9 Custom Programming Blocks

Icon	Name	Description
	My Blocks	A collection of one or more configured programming blocks that are designed to perform a specific action.
	Web Downloads	A My block that someone else has created and which you have downloaded and added to your Lego Mindstorms NXT 2.0 GUI.

click on the Programming pallete's Custom tab and then move the mouse pointer over their icons. Any blocks of these types are then displayed. By default, you don't have any My Block programming blocks. Table 5.9 provides an overview of these blocks and their purpose.

SUMMARY

This chapter provided you with foundational information needed to begin programming using NXT-G. You learned about the execution of computer programs and how NXT-G programs are developed. You were introduced to pseudocode and flowcharts and given examples of these important program planning and design tools. This chapter showed you how to create and switch between different developer profiles and how to open and create NXT-G programs. This chapter also showed where to find programming blocks and reviewed their location on the Programming palette.

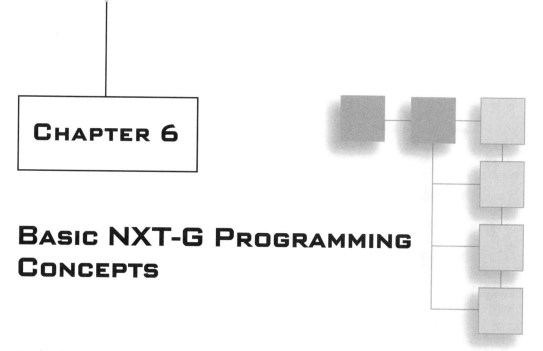

CHAPTER 6

BASIC NXT-G PROGRAMMING CONCEPTS

In the last chapter you learned how to create and open NXT-G programs, and you learned a lot about the various NXT-G programming blocks. Now it is time to dig a little deeper and learn how to use sequence beams to develop NXT-G programs that can run sequentially or that can multitask, executing multiple tasks in parallel. You will learn how to work better in the work area, and you will learn how to add comments to your NXT-G programs in order to document your programming logic.

The major topics covered in this chapter include:

- A breakdown of the different parts of the programming block icons
- Getting to know a little more about the Starting Point
- Learning how to work with sequence beams
- Learning how to multitask using parallel sequence beams
- Adding additional value to your NXT-G programs using comments

DISSECTING PROGRAMMING BLOCKS

Programming blocks define different actions that you can instruct the NXT Brick to execute. Programming blocks have attributes or modifiers that affect their operation. These attributes are displayed in the configuration panel, as shown in Figure 6.1, whenever a programming block is selected. By modifying

Figure 6.1
The configuration panel facilitates the customization of programming block actions.

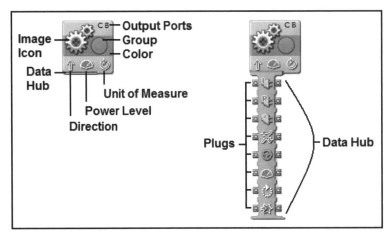

Figure 6.2
A breakdown of the different attribute information displayed on programming blocks.

programming block attributes, you can customize the actions the programming block performs. The configuration panel is only visible when a single programming block is selected. If no programming block is selected or if more than one programming block is selected the configuration panel turns blank.

Changes made to programming block attributes are reflected in the appearance of the blocks. Figure 6.2 demonstrates how much attribute information you can glean from a programming block just by looking at it.

Figure 6.2 provides a detailed example of the attribute information displayed on a typical programming block. In the case of Figure 6.2, a Move block is shown twice, with and without its data hub extended. A *data hub* is a collection of input and output ports that programming blocks can use to receive and transmit data.

You will learn all about the data hub in Chapter 8, "Advanced Programming Techniques."

Hint

You can use data wires, which are introduced in Chapter 8, to pass data between programming blocks, even those located on different sequence beams.

As shown in Figure 6.2, seven distinct pieces of attribute information are visible. Attributes vary from programming block to programming block and not all programming blocks display the same number or type of attribute data. In the case of the Move block shown in Figure 6.2, the block is identified by its image icon. Its direction is set to forward, its power level is set to 75 percent, and its unit measure is set to rotations. In addition, the block is set to control two motors, attached to ports B and C on the NXT Brick. The circular shape and color stripe identifies this block as being a Common programming block. If more information is needed or if you are not sure what a given attribute symbol means, you can either select the programming block and review its attribute data in the configuration panel or you can look the block up in the Lego Mindstorms NXT 2.0 help file.

Beginning at the Starting Point

All NXT-G programs begin at the Starting Point. The Starting Point is an object located on the left side of the work area. Just to the right of the Starting Point is the word Start, as shown in Figure 6.3, marking the point where you place a NXT-G program's first block. The word Start is enclosed by four brackets that outline the shape of a programming block. Programming blocks are connected

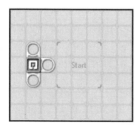

Figure 6.3
Every NXT-G program begins at the Starting Point.

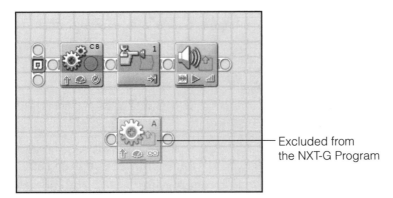

Excluded from
the NXT-G Program

Figure 6.4
Programming blocks not connected to a NXT-G program's sequence beams are not saved as part of the program file.

to the Starting Point via a sequence beam. Programming blocks are downloaded to the NXT Brick when you download your program into it.

Trap

Any blocks that are not connected to a NXT-G program's sequence beams, as demonstrated in Figure 6.4, are not considered to be a part of your NXT-G program. As such, they will not be downloaded to your NXT Brick.

To add a programming block to a NXT-G program, locate the block on the Programming palette, click on it, and hold down the left mouse button. Drag the left mouse button toward a sequence beam. As the programming block approaches the sequence beam, the beam will automatically expand to make room for the block. The location where the block will be placed is identified by three vertical white grid squares as demonstrated in Figure 6.5.

Figure 6.6 demonstrates how the programming block snaps into place when released on top of a sequence beam.

Hint

You can remove a programming block from a sequence beam by selecting it and then pressing the Delete key. If you remove a programming block from a sequence beam, the beam will automatically resize itself to reclaim space formerly allocated to the programming block.

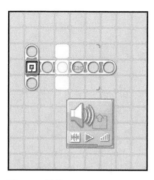

Figure 6.5
The work area displays three vertical white grid squares at the location where the programming block will be positioned.

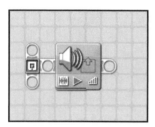

Figure 6.6
Programming blocks automatically snap into place when dropped on a sequence beam.

UNDERSTANDING THE SEQUENCE BEAM

The sequence beam's purpose is to manage the order, or *flow,* in which programming blocks execute in NXT-G programs. To add additional programming blocks to a NXT-G program, you must add them to the sequence beam. Programming blocks are executed in the order, or sequence, in which they are placed on sequence beams.

By default, the sequence beam automatically expands to make room for a new programming block when you drag the block near the beam. This is true whether you drag a programming block to the end, the middle, or the beginning of the sequence beam. Other programming blocks are automatically repositioned as necessary to make room for a new programming block added to the beginning or middle of the sequence beam.

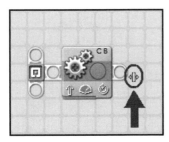

Figure 6.7
When the mouse pointer turns into a pair of arrow-tipped brackets, you can manually adjust a sequence beam's length.

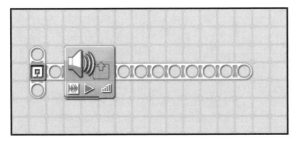

Figure 6.8
An example of a sequence beam that has been manually extended.

If you prefer, you can manually increase the length of sequence beams. To do so, move the mouse pointer over the end of a sequence beam and left click on it. In response, the mouse pointer will turn into a pair of arrow-tipped brackets, as demonstrated in Figure 6.7. Next, drag the mouse pointer outward as you continue to hold down the mouse button. Once you have the sequence beam's length the way you want it, double click on it to lock it in place.

Figure 6.8 shows an example in which a sequence beam has been manually extended several inches.

If you single click as you draw, you can pin the sequence beam to that location on the work area and then continue to draw it in a different direction. You can continue to draw the sequence beam in various directions using this approach.

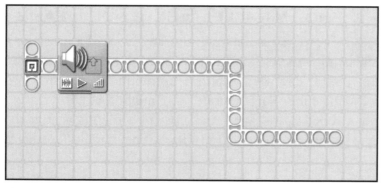

Figure 6.9
An example of a sequence beam that has been manually extended in different directions.

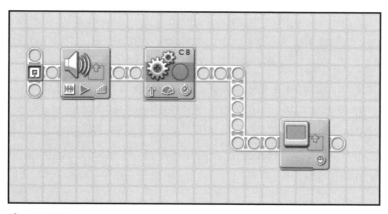

Figure 6.10
An example of an extended beam populated with programming blocks.

When finally done, double click on the new end of the sequence beam to lock it into position, as demonstrated in Figure 6.9.

Once you are done extending a sequence beam, you can go back and add programming blocks to it as needed to develop your NXT-G programs, as shown in Figure 6.10.

MULTITASKING USING PARALLEL SEQUENCE BEAMS

Sometimes executing NXT-G programs one programming block at a time along a single sequence beam is all a robotic creation requires. However, often you need to create programs that enable your creations to multitask, executing two or more actions at the same time. For example, you might want to create a program that will allow a robot to walk and make use of a robotic arm at the same time. NXT-G programs support multitasking using parallel sequence beams.

If you look closely at the Starting Point, you will see that it presents three parallel sequence beams; the one pointing to the right is the one you have seen in use up to this point in the book. The other two sequence beams point up and down. You can use the upper or lower sequence beam to set up parallel processes within your NXT-G programs by moving the mouse pointer over one of these two sequence beams and, while pressing and holding down the left mouse button, move the mouse pointer up or down. Note that when you click on the upper or lower sequence beam, the mouse pointer turns into a reel, as shown in Figure 6.11, to indicate that you can resize the sequence beam.

Once the mouse pointer turns into a reel, you can change a sequence beam's length. Figure 6.12 shows an example where the lower sequence beam has been pulled downward, pinned, pulled to the right, and then pinned again.

Figure 6.13 shows the same NXT-G program once program blocks have been added to the second sequence beam.

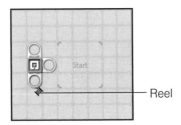

Figure 6.11
The mouse pointer has turned into a reel indicating that you can now grab the sequence beam and resize it.

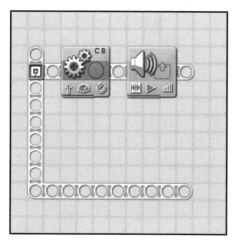

Figure 6.12
An example of a NXT-G program under development that has two sequence beams.

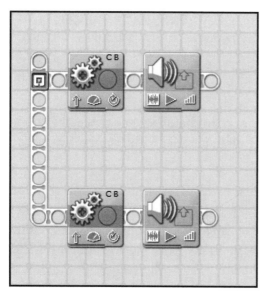

Figure 6.13
This NXT-G program performs two separate sets of actions in parallel within one another.

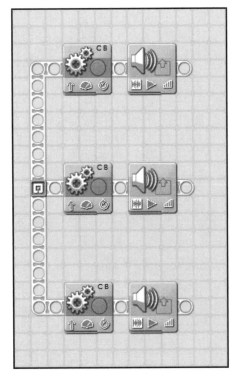

Figure 6.14
This NXT-G program performs three sets of parallel actions.

By expanding and adding programming blocks to the upper sequence beam, you can add a third set of actions that will operate in parallel with the first two sets of actions, as demonstrated in Figure 6.14.

In addition to the parallel sequence beams already available at the Starting Point, you can add new parallel sequence beams at other points along existing sequence beams within your program. This is accomplished by placing the mouse pointer over an open portion of the sequence beam where you want to add a parallel sequence beam and then holding down the Shift key while you move the mouse pointer to draw and expand a new beam originating from the existing beam, as demonstrated in Figure 6.15.

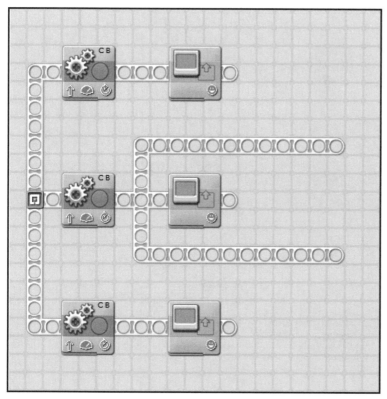

Figure 6.15
In this example, two new sequence beams have been added to the NXT-G program.

Figure 6.16 shows how the NXT-G program shown in Figure 6.15 might look once the program blocks have been added to the new sequence beams.

MOVING PROGRAMMING BLOCKS AROUND YOUR NXT-G PROGRAMS

If you need to move a programming block from one location to another within a NXT-G program, click on the block to select it. When you do this, the block is highlighted and surrounded by a blue square, as shown in Figure 6.17.

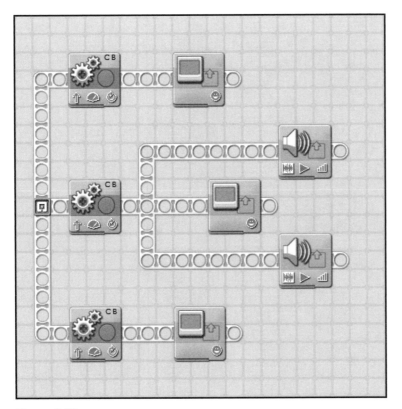

Figure 6.16
An example of a NXT-G program whose programming logic is outlined using five sequence beams.

Once it is selected, left click on the programming block and, while continuing to hold down the left mouse button, drag the programming block to its new location.

Trap

In order to drag and drop a programming block from one location to another, the mouse pointer must be set to the Pointer Tool. As shown in Figure 6.18, the Pointer Tool makes the cursor look like a pointer arrow, which is the default setting for the mouse pointer.

If you need to move more than one contiguous programming block, you can drag and drop them all at once by clicking on the work area and then drawing a blue square around the entire block as demonstrated in Figure 6.19.

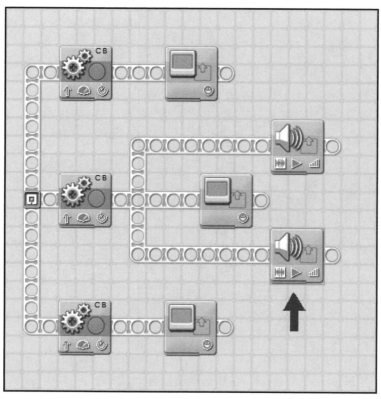

Figure 6.17
The highlighted programming block is the currently selected block.

Pointer Tool

Figure 6.18
The Pointer Tool is selected by default each time you start a new programming project.

Once selected, you can drag and drop the selected programming blocks to their new location by left clicking on one of the blocks, and then holding down the left mouse button while moving them to their new location.

Trick

You can also select multiple programming blocks by selecting the first block and then, while holding down the Shift key, selecting additional programming blocks.

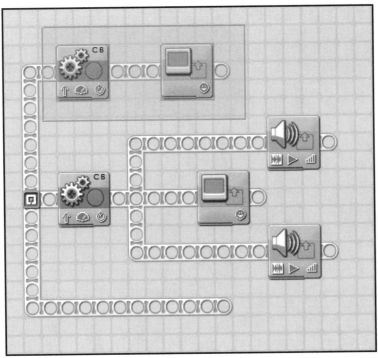

Figure 6.19
An example of a NXT-G program in which two program blocks have been selected.

Trap

If you make any mistakes when moving programming blocks, you can use the toolbar's Undo and Redo commands to put things back to a prior state. You can also use the Cut, Copy, and Paste commands to make copies of programming blocks.

GETTING CONTROL OF THE WORK AREA

Sometime when working on a lengthy NXT-G program you may need to reposition the work area in order to bring the portion of the program you want to work on into view. One option is to use the work area map to move around your program, as was discussed in Chapter 2, "Getting Started." Another option is to use the Pan Tool located in the toolbar, as shown in Figure 6.20.

Pan Tool

Figure 6.20
Using the Pan Tool to drag a new portion of the work area into view.

Once you have selected the Pan Tool, you can use the cursor to click on an open area of the work area and then drag that location to a new position on the screen.

IMPROVING NXT-G PROGRAMS USING COMMENTS

Although working with graphical programming blocks makes programming in NXT-G easier than working with most other programming languages, NXT-G programs can still grow to be very large and complex. The larger and more complex a program gets, the more difficult it is to understand. This makes program maintenance difficult.

As time goes by, it is easy to forget why a given program was designed the way it was. The solution to this dilemma is to add plenty of comments to your NXT-G programs. Comments help explain the logic that is being implemented in your program. This makes the program easier to understand and support, both for you and for anyone else that you share your NXT-G programs with.

Comments give you the opportunity to document what you are doing and why. Use comments to explain the logic behind particularly complicated pieces of programming logic. You'll appreciate the bread crumbs you leave behind should you ever need to return to the NXT-G program to modify it. Comments can also be used to document assumptions that have been made and the intended output and results of your NXT-G program.

Adding Comments to Your NXT-G Programs

To add a comment to your NXT-G program, click on the Comment Tool button located on the toolbar. This button is shaped like a callout balloon as shown in Figure 6.21.

Comment Tool

Figure 6.21
You must click on the Comment Tool in order to add a comment to your NXT-G program.

Once you have selected the Comment Tool button, all you have to do to add a comment to a NXT-G program is click on an open portion of the work area. A white box will appear into which you can begin typing. This space will automatically resize itself to accommodate as much text as you enter. If you press Enter when typing in text, a carriage return is executed, allowing you to continue typing in a new line.

Trick

Once written, you can modify a comment by selecting it, positioning the cursor at the desired location within the comment, and entering your new text.

You can move comments around the work area if you need to by clicking on the Pointer icon in the toolbar and then selecting a comment. When you do this, the comment is enclosed within a blue square. You can drag and drop the comment to a new location on the work area by placing the mouse pointer over a portion of the outlying blue square and holding down the left mouse button to grab onto it.

Comments can be deleted by selecting them and pressing the Delete key.

Figure 6.22 shows an example of a NXT-G program with three programming blocks and corresponding comments. Each comment provides a detailed explanation of the action that the blocks are configured to perform.

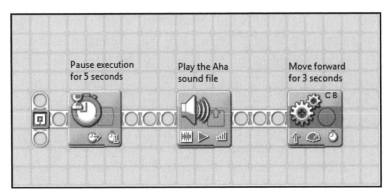

Figure 6.22
An example of a NXT-G program that contains comments describing each programming block's configuration and purpose.

Figure 6.23
Adding a high-level comment to a NXT-G program.

Trick
_____

You can also add a comment by double clicking on a free spot in the work area and then typing in comment text.

_____

You can provide more high-level comprehensive documentation for your NXT-G program by clicking on the Mindstorms icon located on the Starting Point. This displays a scrolling text box labeled Info: at the bottom of the Lego Mindstorms NXT 2.0 GUI (in the location where the configuration panel is displayed) as demonstrated in Figure 6.23.

A good way to make use of the Info: text box is to use it to document your program's name, purpose, creation date, and last update. This way anyone, including yourself, who comes back later and looks at this documentation, can immediately assess the program's purpose, author, and other useful information.

SUMMARY

This chapter showed you how NXT-G reflects programming block configuration through the display of graphic images on the programming block's icon. You learned more about the Starting Point as well as how to work with sequence beams. This included how to develop multitasking programs using parallel sequence beams. You also learned the importance of documenting your NXT-G programs through the addition of comments.

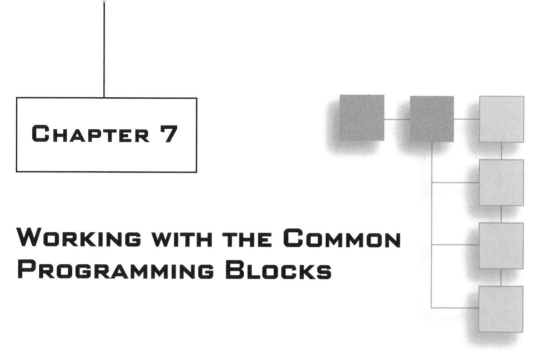

CHAPTER 7

WORKING WITH THE COMMON PROGRAMMING BLOCKS

The seven programming blocks located on the Common palette are the most commonly used programming blocks. A good understanding of how to work with these blocks is essential to your success as a Lego Robotics developer. In this chapter you will review all of the major features and capabilities of these blocks. This will include learning how to work with and configure programming block attributes.

The major topics covered in this chapter include learning how to:

- Move your robots
- Record and play back motor movement
- Play sounds and display graphics on the NXT Brick's LCD
- Pause execution and retrieve sensor data
- Control logic flow using loops and conditional logic

A DETAILED REVIEW OF THE COMMON BLOCKS

The NXT-G programming language consists of dozens of different types of blocks, each of which is designed to perform a different action. Each of these blocks is customizable, allowing you to configure many different details of block executions. Of all the programming blocks, the blocks on the Common palette are by far the most commonly used and therefore merit additional attention. Common programming blocks include all of the following:

- Move
- Record/Play
- Sound
- Display
- Wait
- Loop
- Switch

Together these programming blocks provide the foundational programming logic needed to develop basic NXT-G programs for all types of robotic creations.

THE MOVE BLOCK

The first of the seven sets of programming blocks located on the Common palette is the Move block. The Move block controls the forward and reverse movement of servo motors. The Move block is used to steer robots in straight lines or to move them along a curve.

As shown in Figure 7.1, the icon representing the Move block contains a number of graphic symbols that indicate how some of the block's attributes have been configured.

Figure 7.2 shows the configuration panel for the Move block. As you can see, it includes all of the configuration attributes shown in Figure 7.1, plus several others.

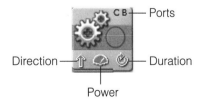

Figure 7.1
The Move block displays four graphic symbols indicating its configuration.

Figure 7.2
The Move block's configuration panel.

Hint

Note that on the far left side of the Move block's configuration panel are feedback boxes. These boxes display data reflecting the movement of servo motors connected to each of NXT Brick's ports. Data is displayed in degrees. To work, you must have at least one servo motor connected to your NXT Brick, and the NXT Brick must be powered on and connected to your computer.

The values shown in each of the three display fields increment or decrement based on whether the servo motors are moved forward or backward. Data is displayed in feedback boxes even if you manually manipulate servo motor movement. By manually moving your robot a predefined distance, for example, and observing the resulting data, you can collect the data needed to precisely configure the duration attribute.

You can reset the value shown in the feedback boxes to zero at any time by clicking on the R button located above the port letter labels.

The Port Attribute

The Port attribute is specified as three check boxes, representing each of the NXT Brick's three servo motor ports (A, B, and C). Ports B and C are selected by default. You can change port settings as needed. You should select a single port in situations where you only need to control one servo motor and that motor is not responsible for moving the robot. This way the block's steering features are not enabled.

You should select two motors for robots that move. Doing so automatically synchronizes the two motors, so that they will move at the exact same speed. Selecting two ports also enables the Steering attribute. If you select all three ports, ports B and C are automatically synchronized.

Trap

If you configure two ports but only attach one servo motor to your robotic creation, the Move block won't work. This is because the block is unable to synchronize the two motors.

If you select all three ports, ports B and C are automatically synchronized, and the servo motor attached to port A must be controlled via another programming block. With this configuration, you must ensure that the servo motors responsible for movement are attached to ports B and C, because the default port assignments cannot be changed.

The Direction Attribute

Direction specifies the direction the robot will move and is configured as forward (default), backward, or stop. Specifying stop resets all configured motors. You may have to reverse the direction setting depending on how you have designed your robot and attached its servo motors. Figure 7.3 depicts the direction that servo motors spin when moving forward and backward.

The Steering Attribute

The Steering attribute is enabled only when two ports are selected. Using the two drop-down selection boxes, you can specify to which side of your robot the two turbo motors are attached. By default, the two motors are configured to move at the same speed, causing the robot to move in a straight line. By adjusting the slider bar, you can make your robot veer to the left or right at various angles.

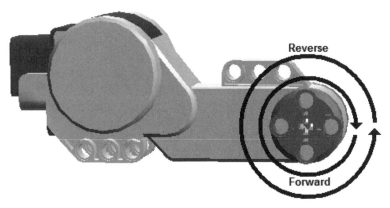

Figure 7.3
A depiction of forward and backward servo motor movement.

The Power Attribute

The Power attribute specifies the power level applied to the servo motors. A range of 0 (no power) to 100 (maximum power) is supported. You can specify the power level either by using the slider control or by typing a numeric value in the text field control. The default power setting is 75.

The Duration Attribute

Duration is specified by first selecting the unit of measure that will be used to control turbo motor movement. Available choices are: unlimited, degrees, rotations (default), and seconds. Unlimited makes the motor(s) run forever. 360 degrees equals one rotation. Seconds specify how long the motors should spin. Once the unit of measure has been specified, choose a numeric value representing how many times the specified unit of measure occurs.

The Next Action Attribute

The Next Action attribute specifies what happens when the robot finishes moving. Two options are available. Selecting Brake instructs the NXT Brick to apply power as necessary to halt the robot immediately. Selecting Coast simply cuts off power to the motor(s) allowing the robot to coast to a stop.

THE RECORD/PLAY BLOCK

The second of the seven sets of programming blocks located on the Common palette is the Record/Play block. The Record/Play block is used to record and play back recorded servo motor movement. As shown in Figure 7.4, the icon representing the Record/Play block contains a single graphic symbol that indicates whether it is configured to record or play servo motor movement.

Figure 7.5 shows the configuration panel for the Move block. As you can see, it includes all of the configuration attributes shown in Figure 7.4, plus several others.

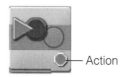

Figure 7.4
The Record/Play block displays a single graphic symbol indicating whether it is currently recording or playing back a recorded action.

Figure 7.5
The Record/Play block's configuration panel.

Figure 7.6
The Sound block displays several graphic symbols indicating how the programming block has been configured.

The Action Attribute

The Action attribute specifies whether the programming block is set to record or play back motor movements. These two mutually exclusive choices are Record (default) and Play. They are selected via radio button.

The Name Attribute

The Name attribute specifies the name of the file in which recorded movement is to be stored or the name of a file in which already recorded movement has been saved. As shown in Figure 7.5, the default file name is RobotAction, but you may change it to anything you wish.

The Recording Attribute

The Recording attribute is enabled only when the Record/Play block's action is set to Record. The Recording attribute is used to specify the output ports that are to be recorded. Ports B and C are recorded by default. Selections are made via check boxes.

The Time Attribute

The Time attribute is enabled only when the Record/Play block's action is set to Record. The Time attribute specifies how many seconds of recording should occur. By default it is set to 30 seconds. Valid entries range from 0 to 2,147,483. You can specify a value either by typing a number into the Time: file or by scrolling up or down using the up and down buttons.

The File Attribute

The File attribute is displayed only when the Record/Play block's action is set to Play. It is enabled only if your NXT Brick is powered on and connected to your computer. It displays a list of previously recorded motor movement files currently stored on the NXT Brick, allowing you to select the movement file that should be played back when the programming block is executed.

THE SOUND BLOCK

The third of the seven sets of programming blocks located on the Common palette is the Sound block. The Sound block is used to play a sound file or to play a musical tone (note). As shown in Figure 7.6, the icon representing the Sound block contains three graphic symbols that indicate some of its configuration settings.

The Sound block's attribute data varies slightly depending on whether the block is configured to play a sound file or tone. Figure 7.7 shows how the configuration panel looks when the Sound block has been configured to play a sound file.

Figure 7.8 shows how the configuration panel looks when the Sound block has been configured to play a note.

Sound files are relatively large files. If your applications play a lot of sounds, you can quickly fill up the NXT Brick's memory. Musical tones, on the other hand, are relatively small and consume a lot less memory. If all your application

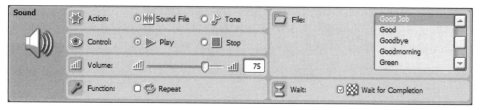

Figure 7.7
The Sound block's configuration panel as it appears when configured to play a sound file.

Figure 7.8
The Sound block's configuration panel as it appears when configured to play a note.

requires is to make a simple sound, playing a tone is the more economical option.

The Action Attribute

The Action attribute is used to specify whether the Sound block plays a sound file (default) or tone. Its value is set via radio button and its assignment determines whether the File or Note attribute is displayed.

The Control Attribute

The Control attribute is used to specify whether the Sound block plays or halts the play of a sound file or tone that may already be in the process of being played by another Sound block.

The Volume Attribute

The Volume attribute determines the volume at which sound files or tones are played. The Volume attribute supports a range of 0 (no volume) to 100 (maximum value) and is expressed as a percentage. The Volume attribute's default setting is 75. Volume can be adjusted by either typing a numeric value in the entry field or by moving the slider bar to the left or right.

The Function Attribute

The Function attribute determines whether the sound file or tone is repeatedly played. By default, the Repeat check box is disabled. As a result, the sound file or tone is played only once. When enabled, the Wait attribute is disabled. Otherwise, the Wait attribute remains enabled.

The File Attribute

When the Sound block is configured to play a sound file, the File attribute is enabled, allowing you to select a sound file from the list of sound files that are

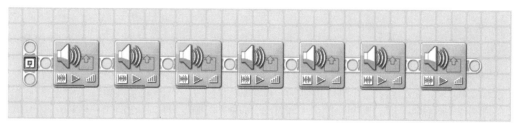

Figure 7.9
An example of a short piece of music consisting of seven notes.

displayed. When you select a file, the file is immediately played on your computer, so you can hear what it sounds like.

The Wait Attribute

The Wait attribute is used to instruct NXT-G to wait until the Sound block has finishing playing before allowing the next block on the sequence beam to execute. This attribute is enabled by default.

The Note Attribute

The Note attribute is accessible only when the Sound block is used to play a tone. As shown in Figure 7.8, a graphical keyboard is displayed in the configuration panel. You can specify the note to be played by using the mouse pointer to click on a keyboard key. A letter representing the selected key is then displayed above the keyboard. To the right of the letter is a field in which you can type a number specifying the number of seconds that the tone should be played.

If you string a number of Sound blocks together on a sequence beam, you can play music. Figure 7.9 shows an example of how this might look.

THE DISPLAY BLOCK

The fourth of the seven sets of programming blocks located on the Common palette is the Display block. The Display block is used to display a graphic, text, or shape on the NXT Brick's LCD. Alternatively, this block can also be used to reset the LCD display, displaying the standard NXT menus.

As shown in Figure 7.10, the icon representing the Display block contains one graphic symbol that indicates the type of resource being displayed.

Figure 7.10
The Display block displays a single graphic symbol indicating the type of resource that it will display when executed.

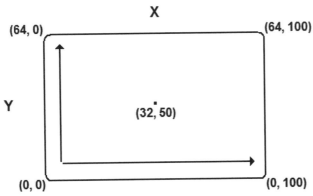

Figure 7.11
A depiction of the system of coordinates used when drawing on the NXT Brick LCD.

Images, text, and shapes are drawn on the NXT Brick LCD using a coordinate system. This system originates from coordinates 0, 0, located in the lower left corner of the display. The Y (vertical) coordinate stretches upward and the X (horizontal) coordinate stretches to the right. Because the LCD is 64 pixels high by 100 pixels wide, the maximum length along the Y coordinate is 64, and the maximum length of the X coordinate is 100. Coordinates 32, 50 specify the center position of the LCD. Figure 7.11 depicts this coordinates system.

Figure 7.12 shows how the configuration panel looks when the Display block is configured to display an image.

Sound files are relatively large files. If your applications play a lot of sounds, you can quickly fill up the NXT Brick's memory. Musical tones, on the other hand, are relatively small and consume a lot less memory. If all your application requires is to make a simple sound, playing a tone is the more efficient option.

Figure 7.12
The Display block's configuration panel as it appears when configured to display an image.

The Action Attribute

The Action attribute specifies whether the block will be used to draw an image, text, or shape on the LCD or whether the LCD screen will be reset, displaying the NXT Brick's menu system.

The Display Attribute

The Display attribute is used to specify whether the Display block clears the LCD area prior to drawing.

Hint

If you do not clear the LCD prior to a drawing operation, you can layer one drawing on top of another, resulting in more complex output, displaying shapes, images, and text at the same time.

The File Attribute

The File attribute is only available when the Display block is used to draw an image. It allows you to select a graphic file containing the image you wish to display.

The Text Attribute

The Text attribute is only available when the Display block is used to write text on the LCD. It allows you to type in the text that you wish to display.

The Type Attribute

The Type attribute is only available when the Display block is used to draw a shape. It allows you to specify the type of shape to draw: Point (default), Line, and Circle.

The Position Attribute

The composition of this attribute varies depending on what is being drawn. If an image is being drawn, a preview of the image is displayed. You can change the location on the LCD where the image is displayed by modifying the X and Y coordinates in the provided entry fields.

If text is being written on the LCD, a preview of the text is displayed. You can change the location where the text is written on the LCD by modifying the X and Y coordinates in the provided entry fields. Alternately, you can specify the line number on which you want the text written. The LCD is capable of displaying up to eight lines of text.

If a shape is being drawn, a preview of the shape is displayed. You can change the location on the LCD where the shape is drawn by modifying the X and Y coordinates in the provided entry fields.

THE WAIT BLOCK

The fifth of the seven sets of programming blocks located on the Common palette is the Wait block. The Wait block is used to either delay execution of programming blocks on sequence beams for a predetermined period of time or to prevent program block execution until data supplied by a sensor satisfies a predetermined condition. There are a total of 12 variations of Wait blocks, which are organized into two categories: Time and Sensor. Six of these are directly accessible from the Common palette. The rest are accessible from within the Wait block's configuration panel.

Figure 7.13 shows what the icons for all 12 variations of the Wait block look like. As you can see, each variation of the Wait block is clearly identified by a different graphic image located in the upper left side of the icon. In addition, the number of graphic configuration symbols displayed on these blocks varies from block to block.

The Wait block's attribute data varies depending on whether it is configured for Time or Sensor. In addition, there are differences in attribute data between different types of sensor configurations. Because there are so many different variations, only two are covered here, the Time and Touch Sensor Wait blocks. A review of these two variations of the Wait block will provide you with a good

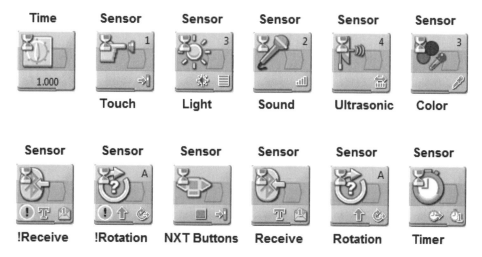

Figure 7.13
The Wait block comes in many different forms.

Figure 7.14
The Wait block's configuration panel as it appears when configured to pause execution a predetermined period of time.

feel for how the other variations work. For additional detail on how to work with all of the various Wait block options, consult the Lego Mindstorms NXT 2.0 Help file.

Configuring the Wait Block to Pause Execution

Figure 7.14 shows how the configuration panel looks when the Wait block has been configured to delay execution for a predetermined period of time.

In this configuration, the Wait block displays the following attributes.

The Control Attribute

When you wish to pause the execution flow along a sequence beam, you must set the Control attribute to Time by selecting that entry from the drop-down list control.

The Until Attribute

The Until attribute specifies the amount of time (in seconds) that execution should be paused on the sequence beam where the Wait block has been placed.

Configuring the Wait Block to Conditionally Pause an Execution Based on Sensor Data

Figure 7.15 shows how the configuration panel looks when the Wait block has been configured to conditional delay execution based on Touch Sensor input data.

In this configuration, the Wait block displays the following four attributes.

The Control Attribute

When you wish to use sensor data to control whether or not execution flow is paused along a sequence beam, you must set the Control attribute to Sensor by selecting that entry from the drop-down list control.

The Sensor Attribute

When configuring the Wait block to use sensor block data, you must specify the source of that data by selecting the appropriate sensor from the drop-down list control. When configuring the Wait block to work with the Touch sensor, this means selecting the Touch Sensor entry.

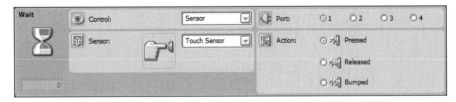

Figure 7.15
The Wait block's configuration panel as it appears when configured to pause execution depending on sensor input data.

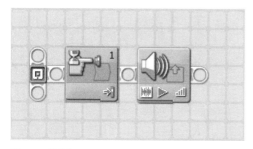

Figure 7.16
In this NXT-G program, execution is delayed until the Touch Sensor is pressed on the robot.

The Port Attribute

In order for the Wait block to retrieve sensor data, it must know which NXT Brick port the sensor has been attached to. This is specified by selecting the corresponding Port attribute radio button control.

The Action Attribute

The Action attribute is used to specify which of three possible sensor states will trigger the Wait block to pause execution along the sequence beam on which it has been placed. These three states include:

- Pressed
- Released
- Bumped

An example of how to work with the Touch Sensor is provided in Figure 7.16. Here, the first block on the sequence beam is a Wait block configured to wait until the touch sensor has been pressed before allowing the remaining Sound block to execute.

THE LOOP BLOCK

The sixth of the seven sets of programming blocks located on the Common palette is the Loop block. The Loop block is a flow control block. It operates by repeating the execution of one or more embedded programming blocks. The Loop block continuously repeats execution of embedded programming blocks until a predefined condition is met.

Figure 7.17
The Loop block is configured by default to repeat its execution forever.

Figure 7.17 shows how the Loop block looks when initially added to a NXT-G program. By default, the Loop block is configured to repeat forever in an endless loop, as indicated by the display of the infinity symbol on the lower right side of the block.

Trap

An endless loop is a loop that does not have a predefined means of terminating its own execution.

The Loop block can be configured to set up five different types of loops, including:

- Forever—Executes forever.
- Sensor—Executes repeatedly until a given sensor value is received.
- Time—Executes repeatedly for a predetermined number of seconds.
- Count—Executes a specific number of times.
- Logic—Executes repeatedly until a logical value of True or False is received from another programming block via a data wire.

Figure 7.18 demonstrates how the Loop block looks when configured to respond to touch sensor input. Specifically, the Loop block repeats its execution until the touch sensor's button is pressed.

Figure 7.19 shows how the configuration panel looks when the Loop block is configured to look for touch sensor input.

The Loop block has five different attributes. These attributes vary depending on the type of loop that has been specified. The configuration panel also displays a

Figure 7.18
This Loop block has been configured to execute until a touch sensor button is pressed.

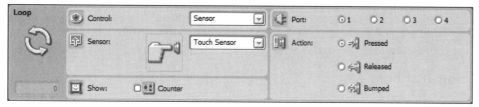

Figure 7.19
The Loop block's configuration panel as it appears when configured to look for touch sensor input.

feedback box for the Loop block, which displays a number representing the number of times the loop has repeated its execution.

The Control Attribute

The Control attribute is used to specify the type of loop that is to be set up (Forever, Sensor, Time, Count, or Logic).

The Sensor Attribute

The Sensor attribute is available only when the Control attribute is set to Sensor. It contains a drop-down list of 11 options, each of which specifies a different type of sensor input. In the case of Figure 7.19, the sensor block has been specified.

The Show Attribute

The Show attribute determines whether or not an output data plug is included as part of the Loop block, allowing the block to pass a number representing the number of times the loop has repeated to another programming block as input.

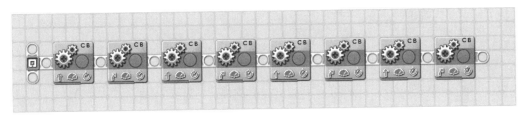

Figure 7.20
An example of a NXT-G program made of eight programming blocks.

The Port Attribute

The Port attribute is available only when the Control attribute is set to Sensor. It is used to identify which port the specified sensor is connected to (1, 2, 3, or 4).

The Action Attribute

The Action attribute is available only when the Control attribute is set to Sensor. Its contents vary depending on which type of sensor the block is configured to work with. In the case of the Touch sensor, you must select from three options (Pressed, Released, and Bumped) in order to specify the condition that will terminate the loop's execution.

A Quick Loop Demonstration

As a demonstration of how loops can be used to streamline NXT-G programs, take a look at the NXT-G program shown in Figure 7.20. Here, the first programming block moves the robot forward, and the second programming blocks moves it a quarter turn to the right. The next two blocks move the robot forward and then to the right again. In like fashion, the next four programming blocks move the robot forward and then to the right. By the time the program has completed, the robot will have moved in a complete square.

A more efficient means of achieving the same results as the NXT-G program shown in Figure 7.20 is to instead use a Loop block as demonstrated in Figure 7.21. Here, only three programming blocks are required to achieve the same result.

THE SWITCH BLOCK

The last of the seven sets of programming blocks located on the Common palette is the Switch block. The Switch block is a flow control block. It is used to

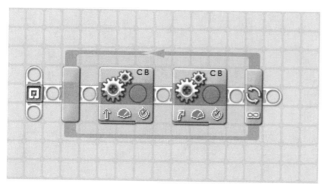

Figure 7.21
An example of a NXT-G program consisting of two programming blocks embedded within a Loop block.

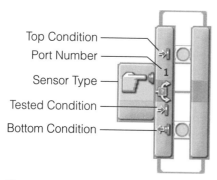

Figure 7.22
The Switch block is configured by default to analyze touch sensor input.

provide NXT-G programs with the ability to select from two sets of paths based on the evaluation of a specified condition.

The Switch block is highly configurable. Figure 7.22 shows how the Switch block looks when initially added to a NXT-G program. By default, the Switch block is configured to evaluate data collected from a touch sensor block.

Figure 7.23 shows the attributes supported by the Switch block when configured to work with a touch sensor. Switch block attributes may vary for other sensors.

Hint

For a detailed review of all the Switch block's attributes, refer to the Lego Mindstorms NXT 2.0 Help file.

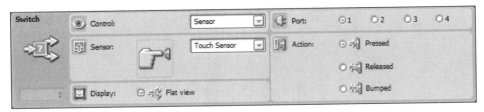

Figure 7.23
An example of the attributes belonging to the Switch block.

The Control Attribute

The Control attribute specifies whether the Switch block tests for an input value or sensor input.

The Sensor Attribute

When the Control attribute is set to Sensor, the Sensor attribute is used to specify which type of sensor the block should work with.

The Display Attribute

The Display attribute controls the appearance of the Switch block. Figure 7.22 demonstrates how the block looks in its default format. As you can see, two sequence beams are visible showing the two paths the Switch block may execute. When the Flat view checkbox control in the Display section of the configuration panel is enabled, the Switch block's appearance changes, showing only one sequence beam at a time, as demonstrated in Figure 7.24. Tabs representing the upper and lower sequence bars control which sequence beam is visible. By default the upper sequence beam is displayed.

Hint

If configured to work with a value instead of a sensor, the Switch block can test for Logic, Number, and Test data passed to the block via data wires. If the data to be tested is a number or text, the Switch block can have more than two sequence beams/tabs.

The Port Attribute

The Port attribute specifies which port on the NXT Brick the sensor is connected to.

Switch block shown in its default view

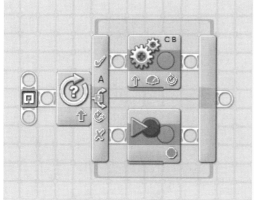

Switch block in flat view mode with the upper beam visible

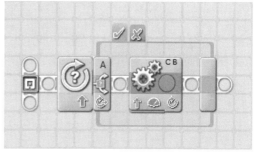

Switch block in flat view mode with the lower beam visible

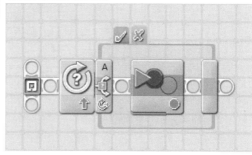

Figure 7.24
A comparison of the regular and flat views of the Switch block.

The Action Attribute

The Action attribute specifies the condition that is to be tested. In the case of the Switch block, the possible conditions are Pressed, Released, or Bumped.

SUMMARY

This chapter provided you with an in-depth review of all of the programming blocks located on the Common palette (Move, Record/Play, Sound, Display, Wait, Loop, and Switch). This included learning how to configure these programming blocks and reviewing their major attributes. An understanding of these programming blocks will enable you to develop NXT-G programs that make robots move, play sounds, display text and graphics on the NXT Brick LCD, collect sensor data, and use that data to control robot actions and behavior.

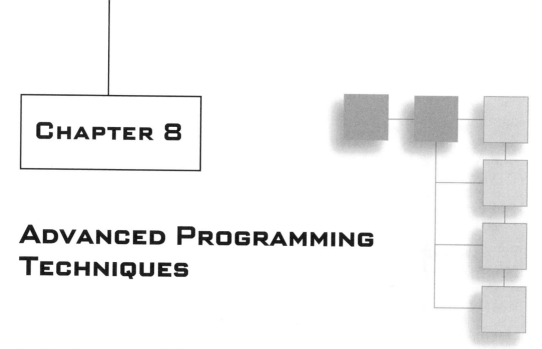

CHAPTER 8

ADVANCED PROGRAMMING TECHNIQUES

In this chapter you will learn advanced NXT-G programming principles. This includes learning more about Action, Sensor, Flow, and Data blocks. You will also learn how to create your own custom blocks. You will learn how to transmit data between programming blocks using data wires. By the time you have completed this chapter, you will have the foundational programming knowledge required to begin developing the NXT-G programs for the robots that you will learn how to build in Chapters 9 through 11.

The major topics covered in this chapter include:

- Learning how to work with data hubs and data wires
- Learning more about programming blocks that pass data through data wires
- Learning how to create custom functions by building My Blocks
- Tips for tracking program execution and locating and fixing errors

PASSING DATA BETWEEN BLOCKS USING DATA WIRES

Using the programming blocks and programming techniques discussed to this point in the book, you have the knowledge required to program simple robots that can move about and make sounds and display LCD text. However, to create robots that can perform specific tasks, interact with their environment, and adjust their operation, you need to learn how to work with data hubs and data wires, using them to pass data between programming blocks. This data can then be analyzed, incorporated into your NXT-G programs, and used to create vastly more complex NXT-G programs and thus more intelligent and capable robots.

With one exception, the Wait programming block, all NXT-G programming blocks are able to communicate and pass data among one another using data wires. Many programming blocks only work properly when you pass data to them through data wires.

Interacting with Data Hubs

A *data hub* is a projection that slides down from the bottom left of a programming block. Some programming blocks automatically display their data hub when added to a NXT-G program, but most blocks keep it hidden by default. To access a programming block's data hub, click on the small tab indentation located at the bottom left edge of the programming block, as demonstrated in Figure 8.1. To hide a data hub, click on the tab located at the bottom of the programming block again.

As shown in Figure 8.1, the data hub contains one or more data plugs. There are two types of data plugs, input and output. Input data plugs are located on the left

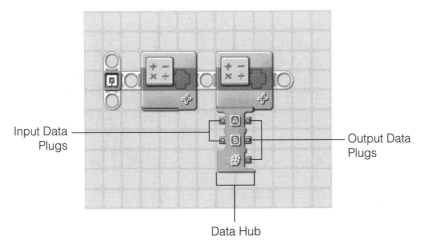

Input Data
Plugs

Output Data
Plugs

Data Hub

Figure 8.1
An example of a Math programming block with its data hub hidden and with it displayed.

side of the data hub and are used to accept data passed to the programming blocks. Output data plugs are located on the right side of the data hub and are used to pass data to other programming blocks.

Connecting Programming Blocks with Data Wires

Data is passed between programming block data hubs by way of data wires. As demonstrated in Figure 8.2, a data wire is a connection between one block's output data plug and another block's input data plug. To draw a data wire from one block to another, move the mouse pointer over the output plug for the block that is to pass the data, making sure that you select the plug associated with the type of data you wish to pass. The mouse pointer will turn into a reel. Left click on the plug to begin drawing the data wire, drag the mouse pointer over to the appropriate input data plug on the other programming block and then release the mouse button.

Hint

To remove a data wire, all you have to do is click on it and press the Delete key.

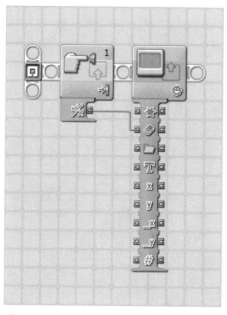

Figure 8.2
An example of two programming blocks connected via a data wire.

Here, logic (True/False) data from a Touch sensor block is passed to a Display block. If a value of True is passed to the Display block, the Display block will clear the NXT Brick's LCD screen. If a value of False is passed to the Display block, the LCD is not cleared.

Different blocks have different numbers of input and output plugs. If you look closely at Figure 8.2, you will notice that there are different graphic symbol labels displayed for each data plug. These symbols provide a visual description of the type of data that the plug is able to work with. In order to create valid connections between different programming blocks, the data wires that connect them must be connected to compatible data plugs. In the case of the example shown in Figure 8.2, the data wire is connected to data plugs that work with logic data on both blocks.

Trick

If you click on a data hubs tab after setting data connections, the data hub is automatically resized so that only the data plugs in use remain displayed as demonstrated in Figure 8.3.

The first two programming blocks show a data wire connected between two data plugs. The second two programming blocks show the same two data plugs after the data hub in the second block has been resized.

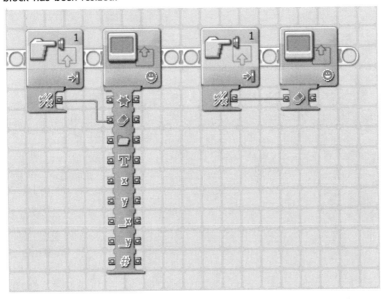

Figure 8.3
An example programming block with its data hub in expanded and collapsed states.

Determining Data Plug Type and Compatibility

In order to create a valid data wire connection between two programming blocks, you must draw a data wire from one block's output plug to the other block's input plug. The two plugs must both support the same data type. Data types include numbers, text, and logic data. To assist you in identifying different types of connections, data wires are color coded, according to the following rules.

- Green data wires pass logic data.

- Yellow data wires pass numeric data.

- Orange data wires pass text.

Every data plug is designed to collect and process a very specific type of data. For example, the Display block shown in Figure 8.2 supports nine different types of input and output plugs. If you position the mouse pointer over the graphic symbol that labels each of these plugs, the plug type is displayed in a popup window.

You can look up detailed information for every plug supported by a programming block by examining that block in the Lego Mindstorms NXT 2.0 Help file. For example, Figure 8.4 shows the table that you will find for the Display block.

Using the information provided in this table, you can identify the type of data that a plug supports. In addition, you can identify the range of data that it supports as well as determine what the value of that data means. To set up a valid data wire, you must connect it between two data plugs that accept the same data type. However, to set up a useful data wire, you must also make sure that the plugs the wire will connect are an appropriate match for the data being passed. In the case of the Display block, this means that when sending X and Y coordinate data, you connect the data wires to the X and Y input data plugs and not to one of the other plugs that also happen to accept numeric data.

Trap

As demonstrated in Figure 8.4, some data plugs accept ranges of data. If data outside of these ranges is passed, an error will occur. The data passed may be ignored, or it may be changed to make it fit the range.

	Plug	Data Type	Possible Range	What the Values Mean	This Plug is Ignored When...
	Action	Number	0 - 5	0 = Image, 1 = Text, 2 = Point, 3 = Line, 4 = Circle, 5 = Restore System Screen	
	Clear	Logic	True/False	True = Clear the screen False = Don't clear the screen	
	Filename	Text	15 character maximum	Filename of image file	Action is not Image
	Text	Text		Text	Action is not Text
	X	Number	0 - 99	X coordinate	
	Y	Number	0 - 63	Y coordinate	
	End point X	Number	0 - 99	End X coordinate (Line only)	Action is not Line
	End point Y	Number	0 - 63	End Y coordinate (Line only)	Action is not Line
	Radius	Number	0 - 120	Radius (Circle only)	Action is not Circle

Figure 8.4
An example taken from the Lego Mindstorms NXT 2.0 Help file for the Display block.

Identifying Broken Data Wires

Sometimes data wires break. A broken data wire is one that is no longer valid. Broken data wires lose their color and turn gray, making them easy to identify. You cannot download NXT-G programs with broken wires into the NXT Brick. Data wires can break for three possible reasons, listed here:

- Missing Input—Occurs when you attach a data wire to an originating programming block that has no input source.

- Too Many Inputs—Occurs when an input plug is configured to receive data from more than one input plug. (Only one input plug is permitted per data wire connection.)

- Data Type Mismatch—Occurs when you attempt to connect a data wire between two incompatible data plug types (for example, an output plug that sends text to an input plug which needs numeric input).

An easy way to determine why a data wire has broken is to move the mouse pointer over the data wire and then look at the Little Help Window, which tells

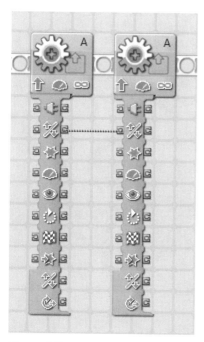

Figure 8.5
An example of a broken data wire with missing input.

you which of the three types of errors has occurred. Figure 8.5 shows an example of a broken data wire that has missing input.

The data wire connection shown in Figure 8.5 begins at an output plug whose corresponding input plug does not have a data source. Figure 8.6 demonstrates that one way of fixing this error is to delete the data wire and redraw it, this time from the same type of data type plug, in this case, the one located at the bottom of the Move block's data hub.

The broken data wire shown in Figure 8.7 has two input sources, which is not permissible.

Figure 8.8 shows an example of a broken data wire with a data type mismatch. Here a data logic output plug on a Touch sensor block has been connected to a Port input plug on a Color Lamp block. The logic plug passes a value of True/False, but the Port plug can only accept numeric data within a range of 1–4.

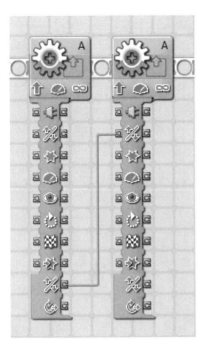

Figure 8.6
The data wire's missing input error has been corrected.

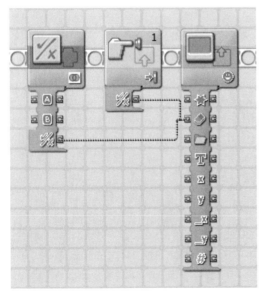

Figure 8.7
An example of a broken data wire with too many inputs.

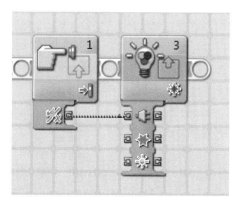

Figure 8.8
An example of a broken data wire with a data type mismatch.

Extending a Data Wire's Path

As data passes through an output plug and a data wire and then to another programming block's input plug, the path that the data travels is referred to as the *wire path*. A wire path can be spread out through multiple programming blocks and data wires. This is achieved by connecting data wires through programming blocks, corresponding input and output data plugs as demonstrated in Figure 8.9.

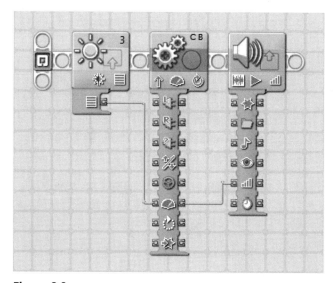

Figure 8.9
An example of a data wire whose path extends through multiple programming blocks.

In Figure 8.9 the power level input and output plug is used to facilitate the creation of the wire path. Here, light intensity data is passed from a Light sensor to a Move block and then on to a Sound block where it is used to configure volume level. The data that traverses the wire path is not changed.

PROGRAMMING BLOCKS THAT USE DATA WIRES

This book has already reviewed in great detail the programming blocks located on the Common palette. These are the same programming blocks that you will find in the Common group on the Complete palette. In addition, you will find instances of Common programming blocks located within other block groups on the Complete palette, where they also logically fit. This chapter reviews a number of the programming blocks found in the Action, Sensor, Flow, Data, and Advanced groups, with particular emphasis on how the blocks work with data wires.

Actions Programming Blocks

The Actions group consists of five programming blocks. Of these, the Sound and Display blocks have already been covered in Chapter 7, "Working with the Common Programming Blocks." These remaining three blocks are discussed in the sections that follow.

The Motor Block

The Motor block is similar to the Move block. Both are designed to control servo motors. However, the Motor block provides more precise control. As shown in Figure 8.10, the Motor block displays information for four attributes: Port, Direction, Power, and Duration.

Figure 8.10
The Motor block provides detailed control over servo motors.

Figure 8.11
The Motor block's configuration panel.

Trap

Avoid using both the Move block and Motor block in the same NXT-G program. Doing so increases the program's size. Specifying one or the other allows for code sharing and means one less block has to be downloaded into the NXT Brick.

Figure 8.11 shows the Motor block's attributes as seen in the configuration panel.

As shown in Figure 8.11, the Motor block supports a total of eight attributes and a Feedback box displays the number of degrees a servo motor has moved. These attributes include:

Port

Specifies the ports the servo motor is connected to (A, B, or C).

Direction

Specifies the direction that the servo motor will rotate (forward, backward, or stop).

Action

Specifies how the servo motor will accelerate: Constant—Immediately accelerates to the specified power level; Ramp Up—Slowly accelerates to the specified power level; Ramp Down—Slowly decelerates to the specified power level.

Power

Specifies the servo motor's power level.

Control

Specifies whether Motor Power is set. If set, Motor Power causes the NXT Brick to attempt to supply whatever level of power is needed to ensure that the servo motor spins at its specified speed (for instance, when operating under adverse conditions).

Duration

Specifies whether servo motor movement should be measured in seconds, degrees, rotations, or unlimited.

Wait

Specifies whether the block should finish its execution before allowing other blocks on the sequence beam to execute.

Next Action

Specifies whether servo motors should brake or coast when the block is done.

The Send Message Block

The Send Message block, shown in Figure 8.12, is used to send messages wirelessly to another NXT Brick via Bluetooth. The Send Message block is designed to work in conjunction with the Receive Message sensor block on another robot. Wireless communications is an advanced topic not covered in this book. For more information, consult the Lego Mindstorms NXT 2.0 Help file.

The Color Lamp Block

The Color Lamp block, shown in Figure 8.13, is one of the simplest programming blocks to use. It controls the color sensor's lamp functionality, enabling the

Figure 8.12
The Send Message block sends wireless messages via Bluetooth to other robots.

Figure 8.13
The Color Lamp block is used to make the Color sensor display a colored light.

display of red, green, or blue light. This block is usually used in pairs, one block turning a light on and the other block turning it off.

The Color Lamp block has the following attributes.

Port

Specifies the port to which the color sensor has been attached.

Action

Specifies whether the lamp features should be enabled or disabled.

Color

Specifies the color of light that should be displayed (red, green, or blue).

Sensor Programming Blocks

As shown in Figure 8.14, the Sensor group consists of nine programming blocks. Sensor blocks retrieve data from different sensors and send that data to other programming blocks that can analyze and act upon it. All sensor blocks pass data through sensor wires. All nine sensor blocks are operated in a similar

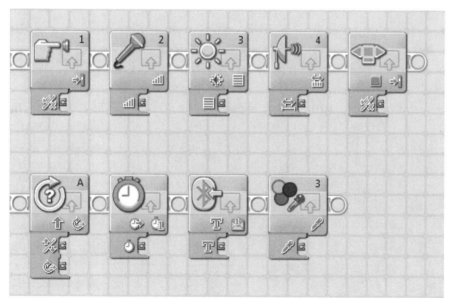

Figure 8.14
There are a total of nine sensor blocks.

Figure 8.15
The Touch sensor block's configuration panel.

manner, having only 2 or 3 attribute settings. This section will use the Touch sensor to demonstrate the operation of all the sensor blocks. To learn more about the other sensor blocks, consult the Lego Mindstorms NXT 2.0 Help file.

The Touch sensor block sends a logic value (True/False) through a data wire that indicates the current status of the Touch sensor. As shown in Figure 8.15, this block has just two attributes, both of which are displayed on its icon.

Port

Specifies the port on the NXT Brick to which the Touch sensor is connected.

Action

Specifies the type of action being tested: Pressed, Released, or Bumped.

To help demonstrate how this sensor block works, look at the example shown in Figure 8.16. Here, the Touch sensor block is used to control the direction in which a robot moves. The Touch sensor control block sends a logical value of True through its data wire when its sensor is pressed, and a False if it is not pressed. The value passed by the Touch sensor block is passed via data wire to

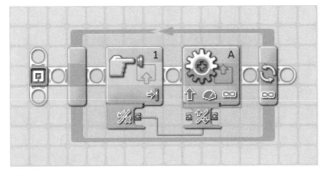

Figure 8.16
A small NXT-G program that uses the Touch sensor to control the robot's direction.

the Motor block's Direction input plug, which accepts logic data and sets the Motor block's Direction attribute. If a True value is received, the Motor block sets the robot's direction to forward. If a False value is received, the robot's direction is set to backward.

Flow Programming Blocks

As their name suggest, Flow programming blocks control the logical execution flow of programming blocks on NXT-G beams. There are a total of four Flow programming blocks. Three of these programming blocks, Wait, Loop, and Switch, are also found on the Common palette and have already been reviewed in depth in Chapter 7. The fourth block is the Stop block. It is arguably the easiest of all the programming blocks to work with. Its sole purpose is to halt a NXT-G program's execution.

The Stop block, shown in Figure 8.17, has no configuration panel and thus has no attributes to configure. The Stop block has a single pair of data plugs, which receive and send logic data. When a value of True is received on its input plug, the block halts program execution. If a value of False is received, program execution continues unaffected.

Data Programming Blocks

Data programming blocks are designed to process data passed to them through data wires and to send output to other programming blocks through their output plugs. There are a total of seven different Data programming blocks, each of which is reviewed in the sections that follow.

The Logic Block

The Logic block, shown in Figure 8.18, performs a logical operation on two input values. The input values can be specified in the block's configuration panel

Figure 8.17
The Stop block is used to halt a NXT-G program's execution.

Figure 8.18
The Logic block performs a logical comparison on its input data.

Figure 8.19
The Logic block's configuration panel.

or supplied via data wire. The Logic block outputs a logical (True/False) value through its output plug.

As shown in Figure 8.19, the Logic block has a single attribute named Operation. In most cases, input values will be passed to the block via data wire. However, you can assign input values of True or False by selecting the check (True) or cross (False) for both of the block's input values on the configuration panel.

In addition, using the drop-down list located in the upper right corner of the configuration panel, you can select one of the four following logical operations that will be used to process the data values.

- **And.** Outputs a value of True if both input values are true.

- **Or.** Outputs a value of True if either or both input values are true (default).

- **Xor.** Outputs a value of True if one input value is True and the other value is False. Outputs a value of False if both input values are True or both input values are False.

Figure 8.20
The Logic block is used to process data from two sensor blocks, and its output is sent to the Move block, where it is used to set the robot's direction.

- **Not.** Inverts a logical value (used when only one value is received as input).

To help demonstrate how this data programming block works, look at the example shown in Figure 8.20. Here, logic data from the Sound and Light sensor blocks is passed to a Logic block where it is analyzed. If either of these sensor block's logic data is True, a value of True is output by the Logic block. When received by the Move block, a value of True sets the robot's direction to forward and a value of False sets the robot's direction to backward.

The Math Block

The Math block, shown in Figure 8.21, performs a mathematical calculation using the two input values passed to the block, as indicated by the graphic symbol displayed on the block's icon. The input values can be specified in the block's configuration panel or supplied via data wire. The Math block outputs the two values as well as a number representing the result of the block's calculation.

As shown in Figure 8.22, the Math block has a single attribute named Operation. In most cases, input values will be passed to the block via data wire. However, you can assign input values by typing values into the A and B entry fields.

Figure 8.21
The Math block performs basic mathematical operations on input data.

Figure 8.22
The Math block's configuration panel.

Using the drop-down list located in the upper right corner of the configuration panel, you can select one of the six following mathematical operations that will be used to process the data values.

- **Addition.** Adds the two numeric values together (default).

- **Subtraction.** Subtracts the second value from the first value.

- **Multiplication.** Multiplies the two numeric values.

- **Division.** Divides the first numeric value by the second numeric value.

- **Absolute Value.** Calculates the absolute value of a single value (used only when the block is given a single value to process).

- **Square Root.** Calculates the square root of a single value (used only when the block is given a single value to process).

The Compare Block

The Compare block, shown in Figure 8.23, determines if one input is greater than, less than, or equal to another input, as indicated by the graphic symbol displayed on the block's icon. The input values can be specified in the block's

Figure 8.23
The Compare block determines if one input is greater than, less than, or equal to another input.

Figure 8.24
The Compare block's configuration panel.

configuration panel or supplied via data wire. The Compare block outputs the two values as well as a logical value representing the result of its comparison.

As shown in Figure 8.24, the Compare block has a single attribute named Operation. In most cases, input values will be passed to the block via data wire. However, you can assign input values in the form of two numbers by typing values into the A and B entry fields.

Using the drop-down list located in the upper right corner of the configuration panel, you can select one of the three following comparison operations that will be used to process the data values.

- **Less Than.** Determines whether the first value is less than the second value (default).

- **Greater Than.** Determines whether the first value is greater than the second value.

- **Equals.** Determines whether the two values are equal.

To help demonstrate how this data programming block works, let's look at the example shown in Figure 8.25. Here, logic data from the Light sensor block is

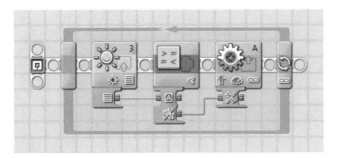

Figure 8.25
The Compare block is used to process data from the Light sensor block, and its output is sent to the Move block, where it is used to set the robot's direction.

Figure 8.26
The Range block determines if a number is inside or outside of a range of numbers.

passed to a Compare block where it is analyzed. If the Light Intensity value supplied by the Light sensor is less than 50, a value of True is sent to the Move block. Otherwise, a value of False is sent. When the Move block receives a value of True through the data wire, it sets the robot's direction to forward. When a value of False is received, the robot's direction is set to backward.

The Range Block

The Range block, shown in Figure 8.26, determines if a number is inside or outside of a range of numbers, as indicated by the graphic symbol displayed on the block's icon. The input value can be specified in the block's configuration panel or supplied via data wire. The Range block outputs the number as well as a logical value representing the result of its comparison.

As shown in Figure 8.27, the Range block has two attributes: Operation and Test value. In most cases, an input value will be passed to the block via data wire.

Figure 8.27
The Range block's configuration panel.

Figure 8.28
The Random block generates a random number within a specified range.

However, you can assign an input value by typing it in the Test value entry field. The range against which the input value is compared can be supplied via data wires (not shown by default on the Range block), or they can be supplied by the Operation attribute. When configuring this attribute, you can choose between determining whether the input value is inside (default) or outside the range. To specify the range, you can either type its upper and lower values in the two entry fields or use the slider control to specify them.

The Random Block

The Random block, shown in Figure 8.28, generates a random number within a specified range. The upper and lower ends of the range can be specified in the block's configuration panel or supplied via data wire. The Range block outputs numbers representing the upper and lower range as well as its randomly generated number from within that range.

As shown in Figure 8.29, the Random block has a single attribute named Range. Minimum and Maximum range values can be passed to the block via data wire, or they can be specified as part of the Range attribute by typing them into the A and B entry fields. Alternatively, these values can be specified using the slider control located beneath the entry fields.

Figure 8.29
The Random block's configuration panel.

Figure 8.30
The Variable block retrieves or modifies a value stored in computer memory.

The Variable Block

The Variable block, shown in Figure 8.30, retrieves or modifies a text, string, or logical value stored in computer memory. A *variable* is a value stored in the NXT Brick's memory. Each Variable block displays the name of the variable that it is configured to work with. In addition, a graphic symbol displayed on the block indicates whether is has been configured to read a variable value from memory or write it to memory. As shown in Figure 8.30, the Variable block data hub displays an output plug when configured to read a variable. However, when configured to write to a variable, it displays both an input and an output plug, allowing the variable's new value to be passed to the block via data wire.

Before a variable can be used in your NXT-G program, you must first define it. To define a variable, you must click on Edit > Define Variables. This displays the Edit Variables window shown in Figure 8.31. This window can also be used to delete variables.

As shown in Figure 8.31, every variable that you define must be assigned a unique name and a data type. In addition, there are three default variables that are always available. These variables are named Logic 1, Number 1, and Text 1. To define a new variable, click on the Create button. Next, type a descriptive name for the variable in the Name field and then, using the drop-down list in the Datatype field, specify the variable's data type. Click on Close when done.

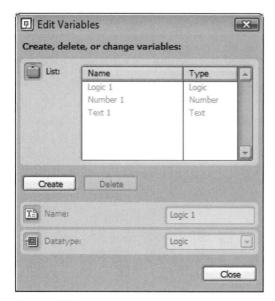

Figure 8.31
New variables are defined from within the Edit Variables window.

Figure 8.32
The Variable block's configuration panel.

It should be noted that variables exist only in the NXT Brick's memory. When the NXT Brick is turned off, the variable is deleted from memory and you will have to define it again to use it.

Once defined, you can use the Variable block to assign a value to the variable and to retrieve that value. Figure 8.32 shows the configuration panel for the Variable block. Three attributes, described below, are available.

List

Lists all available variables and allows you to select one.

Action

Specifies whether the block will be used to read the variable's value or to write a new value in memory for the variable.

Value

The Value attribute is accessible only when the Action attribute is set to Write. It allows you to assign a value of True or False to a logic variable, a number to a numeric variable, or to enter a text string to be assigned to a text variable.

The Constant Block

The Constant block, shown in Figure 8.33, retrieves or modifies a text, string, or logical value stored in computer memory. A *constant* is a value stored in the NXT Brick's memory that, unlike a variable, never changes. Each Constant block displays the name of the constant that it is configured to work with. The Constant block data hub has an output plug. A graphic symbol is displayed on the hub indicating the constant's data type.

Before a constant can be used in your NXT-G programs, you must first define it. To define a constant, you must click on Edit > Define Constants. This displays the Edit Constants window shown in Figure 8.34. This window can also be used to edit and delete constants.

As shown in Figure 8.34, every constant that you define must be assigned a unique name and a data type. To define a new constant, click on the Create button and type a descriptive name for the constant in the Name field and then, using the drop-down list in the Datatype field, specify the variable's data type (Logic, Number, or Text), and then specify the constant's value in the Value section. Click on Close when done.

Figure 8.33
The Constant block retrieves a constant value stored in computer memory.

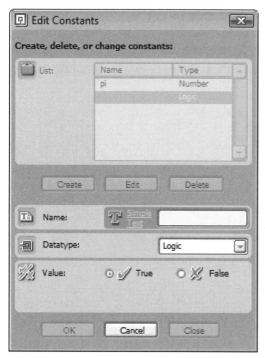

Figure 8.34
New constants are defined from within the Edit Constants window.

Figure 8.35
The Constant block's configuration panel.

You can use the Constant block to retrieve the value assigned to the constant whenever you need it. Figure 8.35 shows the configuration panel for the Constant block. Four attributes, described below, are available.

Action

The Action attributes allow you to either choose the constant you want to work with from a list of existing constants or to use the block to define a new constant.

Data Type

The Data Type attribute, available only when using the block to define a new constant, is used to specify either Logic, Number, or Text as the constant's data type.

Value

The Value attribute, available only when using the block to define a new constant, allows you to specify a value for the constant.

Name

The Name attribute, available only when using the block to define a new constant, allows you to assign a name to the new constant.

Advanced Programming Blocks

Advanced programming blocks represent programming blocks that do not fit into any previously discussed block groups. They perform a range of different functions. There are a total of seven Advanced programming blocks, each of which is reviewed in the sections that follow.

The Number to Text Block

The Number to Text block, shown in Figure 8.36, converts a numeric value to a text value, allowing it to be displayed on the NXT Brick's LCD. The input value can be specified in the block's configuration panel or supplied via data wire. The Number to Text outputs two values, the number that needs to be converted and the text string version of that number.

Figure 8.36
The Number to Text block converts a number to a text string allowing it to be displayed on the NXT Brick's LCD.

As shown in Figure 8.37, the Number to Text block has a single attribute named Number. Normally, the number that the block converts into text is passed to it via data wire. Alternatively, you can specify the number to be converted by typing it into the Number entry field.

The Text Block

The Text block, shown in Figure 8.38, concatenates up to three strings together, creating a new longer string. The input values can be specified in the block's configuration panel or supplied via data wire. The block outputs up to four values, the source text strings, and the resulting concatenated text string.

As shown in Figure 8.39, the Text block has a single attribute named Text. Normally, the text strings that the block concatenates together will be passed to

Figure 8.37
The Number to Text block's configuration panel.

Figure 8.38
The Text block concatenates up to three strings together to create a larger string.

Figure 8.39
The Text block's configuration panel.

it via data wire. However, you can specify the text strings by typing them into the three text fields labeled A, B, and C.

The Keep Alive Block

The Keep Alive block is used to override the NXT Brick's automatic sleep mode, which puts the NXT Brick to sleep after a period of inactivity resulting from non-use. See Figure 8.40.

Unlike the other Advanced programming blocks, the Keep Alive block does not have any attributes to configure.

The File Access Block

The File Access block writes or reads numeric or text data files on the NXT Brick. The File Access block works similarly to the Variable block, except that instead of storing data in memory, the data is stored in a file, allowing it to be stored indefinitely. On the down side, storing data in files consumes more of the NXT Brick's available storage space.

As shown in Figure 8.41, graphics symbols that indicate the type of data being worked with are displayed on the File Access block. The symbols also indicate whether the block has been configured to read or write data.

Figure 8.40
The Keep Alive block prevents the NXT Brick from entering Sleep Mode.

Figure 8.41
The File Access block writes and reads data from files stored on the NXT Brick.

Figure 8.42
The File Access block's configuration panel.

Figure 8.42 shows the configuration panel for the File Access block. Its attributes are described below.

Action

The Action attribute specifies the actions performed by the block. Available choices include:

- **Read**—Reads the data stored in the specified file.
- **Write**—Writes data to the specified file. If the target file already contains data, the new data is written to the end of the existing file.
- **Close**—Closes a file after it has been written to or read from.
- **Delete**—Deletes the file.

Hint

You must use the Close action after each time you perform an action on a file. For example, if you write something to a file, you have to close it before you can read from it. You will need to add a different File Access block to your NXT-G program for each action you perform.

Name

The Name attribute is used to specify the name of the data file that will be created, processed, deleted, or closed.

File

The File attribute is available only when your NXT Brick is connected to your computer. It allows you to select an existing file stored on your NXT Brick.

Type

The Type attribute is used to specify the type of data in use (text or numeric).

Text

Although when writing to a file the data to be written is usually supplied via data wire, you can specify the data to be written by keying it into the entry field for the Text attribute. The Text attribute is available only when the Action is set to Write.

The Calibrate Block

The Calibrate block is used to calibrate the sound and light sensors. Its value is represented as a percentage between 0 and 100. As demonstrated in Figure 8.43, symbols displayed on the Calibrate block indentify whether it has been configured to work with the light or sound sensor as well as whether the block has been configured to set the minimum or maximum value.

Hint

In addition to calibrating sensors using the Calibrate block, you can also calibrate sensors from the Lego Mindstorms NXT 2.0 GUI, as described in Chapter 2, "Getting Started."

Figure 8.44 shows the configuration panel for the Calibrate block. Its attributes are described below.

Figure 8.43
The Calibrate block is used to calibrate sound and light sensors.

Figure 8.44
The Calibrate block's configuration panel.

Port

The Port attribute specifies the port on the NXT Brick to which the sensor being configured has been attached (1, 2, 3, or 4).

Sensor

The Sensor attribute specifies whether the programming block is to be used to calibrate a light or sound sensor.

Action

The Action attribute is used to specify whether the block will calibrate or delete the specified sensor. Deleting a sensor simply restores its default settings.

Value

The Value attribute is used to specify either the minimum (0) or maximum (100) value.

The Reset Motor Block

The Reset Motor block, shown in Figure 8.45, is used to reset the servo motor's automatic error correction feature. Text displayed in the upper right corner of the Reset Motor block shows the ports on which the block will perform the reset. Although not shown by default, this block's data hub has three input and output data plugs that can be used to receive and send the port assignments of the servo motors.

Figure 8.46 shows the configuration panel for the Reset Motor block. As you can see, it contains a single attribute named Port, which is used to specify on which port (A, B, or C) the reset action should take place.

Figure 8.45
The Reset Motor block disables automatic error correction for servo motors.

Figure 8.46
The Reset Motor block's configuration panel.

Figure 8.47
The Bluetooth Connection block is used to establish a Bluetooth connection with another Bluetooth device.

This programming block is seldom used. However, it can be helpful in situations where the Move or Motor blocks have been configured to set the servo motors to coast to a stop. In these situations the servo motor's automatic error correction should accurately keep track of motor movement. However, if you need to, you can use the Reset Motor block to stop automatic correction.

The Bluetooth Connection Block

The Bluetooth Connection block, shown in Figure 8.47 is used to establish a connection with another Bluetooth device, such as another NXT Brick. To learn more about this feature, consult the Lego Mindstorms NXT 2.0 Help file.

CREATING CUSTOM FUNCTIONS BY CREATING MY BLOCKS

As you gain additional experience developing NXT-G programs for your robots, you may often find yourself repeatedly working with and configuring certain groups or programming blocks in the same way over and over again. This is not an efficient use of time or energy. A better solution is to develop a custom My Block made up of these programming blocks and then add the My Block to your NXT-G programs whenever you need to perform whatever task(s) those programming blocks are designed to manage. In this way, you can create a personal library of custom functions, each of which performs a specific task, allowing you to quickly assemble new NXT-G programs without having to continuously reinvent the wheel. My Blocks can also be used to hide complexity in your NXT-G programs.

My Blocks are stored and managed on the Custom palette. They exist in two forms: My Blocks and Web Blocks. A *My Block* is a collection of one or more customized programming blocks that perform a specific task. A *Web Block* is a

My Block that someone else has developed and which you have downloaded from the Internet, allowing you to leverage someone's programming knowledge and experience. Lego Mindstorms NXT 2.0 does not come with any My Blocks or Web Blocks.

Creating and Managing My Blocks

My Blocks are nothing more than collections of programming blocks that you configure to perform a specific action and then save as a reusable unit in the form of a new programming block. Once created, My Blocks can be added to a NXT-G program just like any other programming block.

Creating a My Block

To create a My Block, add and configure the programming blocks you want to use to the work area. For example, you might create a My Block using the programming blocks shown in Figure 8.48.

Once you have finished configuring the programming blocks, select them and either click on the Create My Block toolbar button or click on Edit > Make A New My Block. In response, the My Block Builder window appears. Assign a descriptive name to the block by filling in the Block Name field and then document the block's function and purpose in the Block Description text field as demonstrated in Figure 8.49.

When done, click on Next and the My Block Builder window will help you create a custom icon for the My Block. The bottom part of the window displays a list of icons that you can drag to the Icon Builder entry field at the top of the window. You can resize the icon by clicking one of the four squares located at

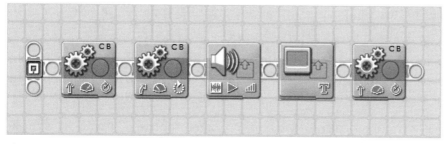

Figure 8.48
A collection of programming blocks to be used as the basis for creating a My Block.

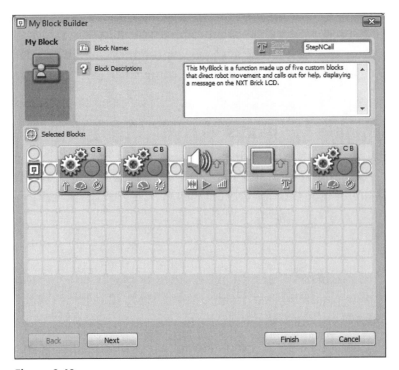

Figure 8.49
The My Block Builder window displays the selected programming blocks and allows you to name and describe the My Block.

the four corners of the icon. A preview of how the My Block's icon will look, located in the top right corner of the window, is immediately updated. You may drag and drop more than one icon onto the Icon Builder entry field, as demonstrated in Figure 8.50.

Once you are done configuring the appearance of your My Block, click on Finish.

The programming blocks that make up the My Block are then removed from the work area and replaced with the new My Block, as demonstrated in Figure 8.51.

The My Block is automatically added to the Custom palette. To view it, simply move the mouse pointer over the My Block icon, as demonstrated in Figure 8.52.

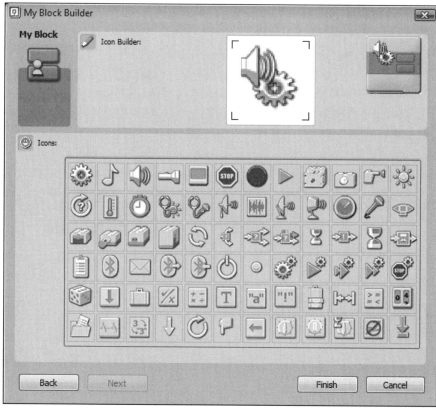

Figure 8.50
You can add and configure one or more icons to the Icon Builder entry area in order to configure the appearance of your My Block.

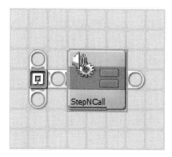

Figure 8.51
Once completed, the My Block is displayed in place of the programming blocks that comprise it.

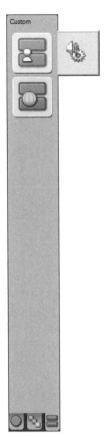

Figure 8.52
The My Block is made visible on the My Blocks group on the Custom palette.

Modifying a My Block

If you decide you need to make a change to a My Block, you may do so by adding it to the work area and either double clicking it or selecting it and then clicking on Edit > Edit Selected My Block. In response, the contents of the My Block are displayed in their own tabbed window in the work area. Make any required changes to the programming blocks that make up the My Block and then close its tabbed window. Click on Yes when prompted to save your changes.

You can also modify a My Blocks icon by selecting it and then clicking on Edit > Edit My Block Icon. My Blocks are stored in their own folder as files with an .rbt file extension. You can delete a My Block by selecting it and then clicking on

Edit > Manage Custom Palette. This will display a window containing two folders, one for your My Blocks and one for your Web Blocks. Open the My Blocks folder, select your My Block file and then press the Delete key to delete it.

Sharing Your My Blocks

If you want, you can take a copy of the My Block file and share it with others, from your Web site, for example. Any My Blocks that you share in this manner will be regarded as Web Blocks by others who download and add them to their Lego Mindstorms NXT 2.0 development environment. To share a My Block, add it to the work area and then click on Edit > Manage Custom Palette. Locate and open the My Blocks folder and then make a copy of My Block and you are ready to share it.

Deleting a My Block

To delete a My Block, add it to the work area and then click on Edit > Manage Custom Palette. Locate and open the My Blocks folder, select the My Block, and press the Delete key. If you delete a My Block, you must then go back and modify any NXT-G programs that made use of it. Otherwise, those programs won't work any more. Figure 8.53 shows an example of what a broken My Block looks like.

Downloading and Installing Web Blocks

As has been stated, a Web Block is just a My Block that you have gotten from somebody else, downloading it from the Internet, for example. Once you have downloaded a Web Block from the Internet, all you have to do to begin working with it is to add it to your Lego Mindstorms NXT 2.0 working environment. To do so, click on Edit > Manage Custom Palette and open the Web Blocks folder

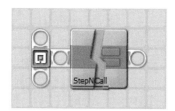

Figure 8.53
An example of a broken My Block.

that is displayed. Drag and drop your new Web Block(s) into this folder and close it.

The next time you place the mouse pointer over the Web Blocks group on the Custom palette, your new Web Blocks will be displayed, and you can begin working with them.

DEBUGGING YOUR NXT-G PROGRAMS

Beginning in Chapter 9, "Go Bot," and going to the end of this book, you will begin developing robots and the NXT-G programs that make them work. As you do so, you may run into occasional problems. Most of the time, all you will have to do to locate and fix programs is carefully review your programming blocks and look for your mistake. Sometimes, however, mistakes are not easy to find. In these situations, you need to do a little debugging.

First and foremost, your NXT-G programs won't download to your NXT Brick if they contain certain types of errors. These errors include:

- Broken data wires
- Broken data blocks

You will have to identify and fix both of these types of errors before you can download and test your NXT-G programs. In addition, sometimes programming blocks are accidentally removed from a NXT program's sequence beams. Any program blocks not connected to sequence beams are not downloaded to the NXT Brick. Check your programs for disconnected programming blocks, and reconnect or remove them as appropriate.

Once you have downloaded your program to your NXT Brick, you can run, test, and debug them. Debugging is the process of locating and fixing errors that occur within computer programs. Unlike some programming languages, NXT-G does not have a built-in debugging tool. However, there are a few simple tricks that you can employ to help you when trying to locate where errors are occurring within your NXT-G programs. For starters, you can embed extra Sound blocks at strategic points within your programs and configure those blocks to play tones so that you know when different parts of your NXT-G programs are executing. Using this approach, you may be able to determine the part of your NXT-G program where an error is hidden, just by watching your robot run and listening for the tones that tell you when different parts of your NXT-G programs are executing.

In a similar fashion, you can embed extra Display blocks within your NXT-G programs when you are developing them and use those blocks to display relevant information when your NXT-G programs run. Information that is displayed might include data that is passed between blocks via data wires or messages that indicate variable values. You can also use Display blocks in place of Sound blocks to identify when different parts of your NXT-G programs execute.

Another way to determine what is going on as your robots run is to leave your robot's NXT Bricks attached to your computer when it runs. This allows you to monitor feedback boxes belonging to programming blocks.

SUMMARY

This chapter rounded out your NXT-G programming foundation by completing your review of NXT-G programming blocks, including those in the Action, Sensor, Flow, and Data groups. You learned how to transmit data through these programming blocks using data hubs and data wires. You also learned how to create custom functions that facilitate code reuse through the development of My Blocks. Lastly, you learned a few tricks for tracking programming execution and locating and fixing program errors. You are now ready to begin developing the NXT-G programs needed to automate the operation of the robots whose development is covered in Chapters 9 through 11.

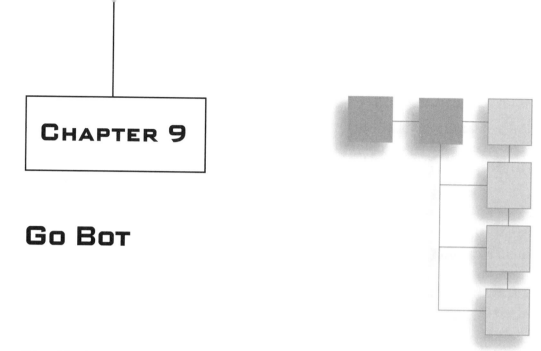

CHAPTER 9

Go Bot

Now it's time to put everything you have learned so far in this book to good use. In this chapter you will learn how to create your first robotic project, the Go Bot, a four-wheeled robot. It uses two servo motors to drive it. It will be programmed to move forward and backward, talk, and display friendly text messages. Go Bot is a great first robotic development project, providing an effective example of the fundamental steps involved in robotic development. It will also provide you with the opportunity to put your programming skills to good use.

The major topics covered in this chapter include:

- Developing a basic understanding of how to create modular robots.
- A review of Go Bot's features and capabilities.
- Step-by-step instructions for building Go Bot.
- Learning how to remote control Go Bot.
- A complete review of the NXT-G program that makes Go Bot come to life.

ROBOTIC DEVELOPMENT METHODOLOGY

Robotic development is usually completed through a series of steps, beginning with design, then assembly, and, finally, programming and testing. In each chapter that follows, you will be presented with a brief introduction that provides a high-level overview and design of a different robot.

More often than not, development involves a lot of experimentation and plenty of mistakes, corrections, and modifications. As you work, make sure that you build structures that are strong and functional. In addition, approach development in a modular manner by breaking down your robots into a series of distinct subassemblies that, when put together, make up your robot. Once assembly is completed, you will wrap things up by programming and then testing your robot.

Hint

When you're done with a robot that you are proud of, it's a good idea to document what you have accomplished. This can be done as easily as snapping a picture of your robot, or it can be as complex as developing a complete set of build instructions, which you can create using various CAD programs like the Lego Digital Designer or LDRAW. You might even consider creating a video of your robot's assembly and operation.

INTRODUCING GO BOT

Moving vehicles are a popular type of robot and make for an excellent starting point. Go Bot is such a robot. As shown in Figure 9.1, Go Bot is a four-wheeled robotic vehicle. The two front wheels are connected to and operated by servo motors and are responsible for the vehicle's propulsion. The back two wheels provide additional support.

Go Bot will be programmed to begin by saying and displaying the word Hello on the NXT Brick's LCD. Next it will play a tone, move forward, pause, and play another tone. Go Bot will then move backward to its starting point, play a tone, and spin in place before saying Goodbye and halting.

Hint

The Go Bot can be used as the basis for creating all sorts of other vehicles. It will serve as the starting point for the robotic projects in Chapters 10 and 11.

Figure 9.1
The Go Bot is a four-wheeled robotic vehicle.

Building Go Bot

Go Bot is a relatively simple and straightforward robotic project. You will create it in six high level steps as outlined below.

- Preparing the NXT Brick
- Assembling the left motor drive
- Assembling the right motor drive
- Assembling the rear wheel chassis
- Assembling Go Bot
- Programming and testing Go Bot

Figure 9.2 provides a complete listing of all the different electronic components and parts needed to make Go Bot. Begin your work on this project by retrieving these pieces from your Lego Mindstorms NXT 2.0 kit and setting them aside to work with.

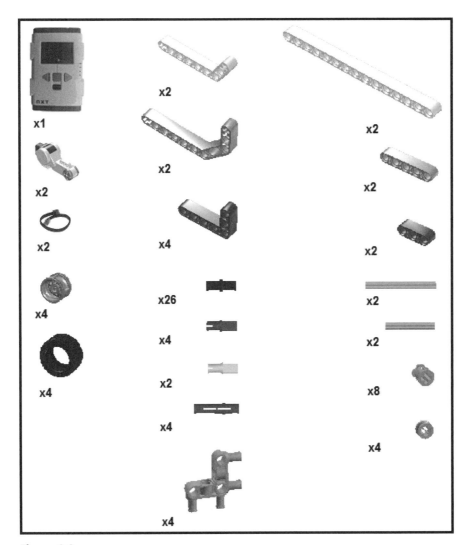

Figure 9.2
The parts inventory list for Go Bot.

Preparing the NXT Brick

Begin the development of Go Bot by preparing the NXT Brick. This involves the attachment of several pieces to the NXT Brick. This facilitates the connection of the servo motor assemblies that will be created in Steps 2 and 3 and then added to the NXT Brick in Step 5.

Step 1—Take two 5M straight beams, four connector peg with friction 3M pegs, and two 3 × 5M perpendicular beams and connect them as shown in Figure 9.3.

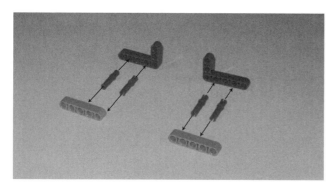

Figure 9.3

Step 2—Take the components created in Step 1 and connect them to the NXT Brick as shown in Figure 9.4.

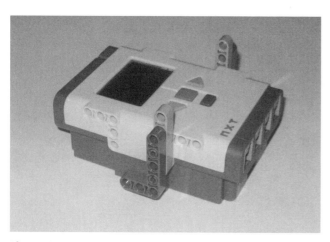

Figure 9.4

Assembling the Left Motor Drive

Now it is time to begin working on Go Bot's servo drive assemblies, beginning with the left motor drive. This is accomplished in four steps.

Step 1—Create the robot's left wheel by connecting a rim to a tire as shown in Figure 9.5.

Figure 9.5

Step 2—Connect one connector peg with friction and cross axles and six connector pegs with friction to one of the servo motors as shown in Figure 9.6.

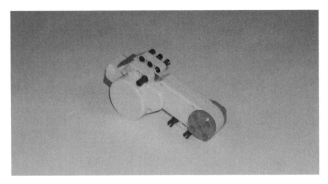

Figure 9.6

Step 3—Connect the completed wheel to the servo motor using one 7M cross axle and two bushings as shown in Figure 9.7.

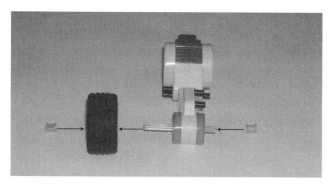

Figure 9.7

Step 4—Connect two connector pegs with friction to a 3×7 double broken angle beam, as shown in Figure 9.8, and then connect the double broken angle beam to the servo motor as also shown in Figure 9.8.

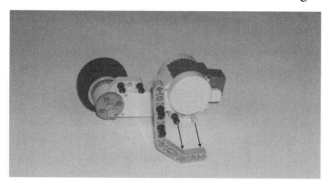

Figure 9.8

Hint

The completed left motor drive should look like the example shown in Figure 9.9.

Figure 9.9

Assembling the Right Motor Drive

The steps required to create the right motor drive assembly closely mirror the steps that you followed to assemble the left motor assembly and are accomplished in four steps.

Step 1—Create the robot's right wheel by connecting a rim to a tire as shown in Figure 9.10.

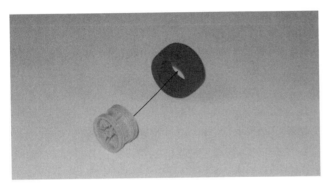

Figure 9.10

Step 2—Connect one connector peg with friction and cross axles and six connector pegs with friction to one of the robot's servo motors as shown in Figure 9.11.

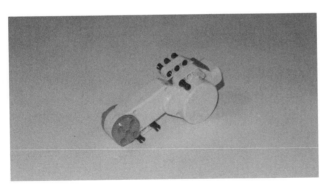

Figure 9.11

Step 3—Connect the completed wheel to the servo motor using one 7M cross axle and two bushings as shown in Figure 9.12.

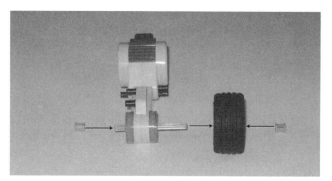

Figure 9.12

Step 4—Connect two connector pegs with friction to a 3 × 7 double broken angle beam, as shown in Figure 9.13, and then connect the double broken angle beam to the servo motor, as also shown in Figure 9.13.

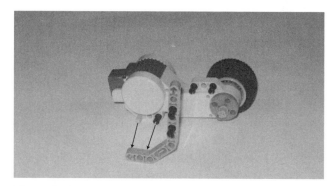

Figure 9.13

Hint
_____

The completed right motor drive should look like the example shown in Figure 9.14.

Figure 9.14

Assembling the Rear Wheel Chassis

With the NXT Brick now prepared and the Go Bot's left and right servo motor assemblies complete, it's time to create the robot's rear wheel chassis. This will be accomplished in four steps.

Step 1—Connect two 15M straight beams and two 3 × 7 angle beams using four pegged perpendicular block 5M pieces as shown in Figure 9.15. Make sure that when connecting the pegged perpendicular block 5M pieces to the 15M straight beams that you insert the peg ends of the pegged perpendicular block 5M pieces into the first and third holes on each end of the 15M straight beam.

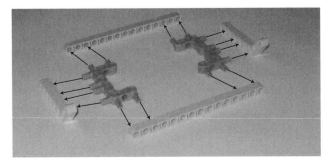

Figure 9.15

Step 2—Connect two 3×5M perpendicular beams to the upper left and right ends of the chassis using a connector peg with friction and connector peg with friction and cross axle, as shown in Figure 9.16.

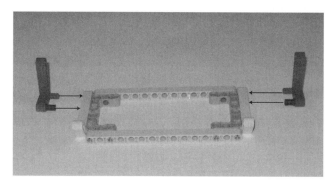

Figure 9.16

Step 3—Connect a 3M straight beam to the left side of the rear chassis using a connector peg with friction and connector peg with friction and cross axle, as shown in Figure 9.17. Add a second 3M straight beam to the right side of the rear chassis using a second connector peg with friction and connector peg with friction and cross axle (not shown in Figure 9.17).

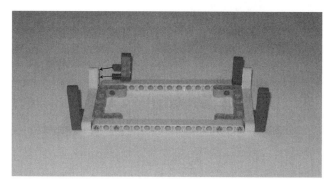

Figure 9.17

Step 4—Assemble a new wheel using a rim and tire and add the wheel to the rear chassis using a 5M cross axle, two bushings, and two half-bushings as shown in Figure 9.18.

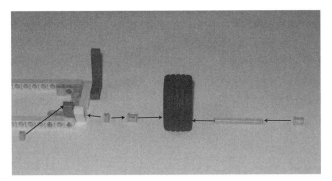

Figure 9.18

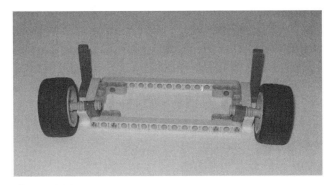
Assembling Go Bot

Now that all of the major subassemblies that make up Go Bot have been put together, it is time to assemble these subassemblies into a completed robot.

Step 1—Attach the left and right servo motor assemblies to the NXT Brick, as shown in Figure 9.20.

Figure 9.20

Step 2—As shown in Figure 9.21, connect the robot's rear wheel chassis to the robot by connecting its $3 \times 5M$ perpendicular beam to the left and right servo motors using the two sets of connector pegs with friction that are already connected to the servo motors.

Figure 9.21

Hint

A fully assembled copy of Go Bot is shown in Figure 9.22.

Figure 9.22

Step 3—To operate, the robot's two servo motors must be connected to the NXT Brick. Set this up by connecting the left servo motor to the NXT Brick's C port and the right servo motor to the NXT Brick's B port using a pair of 35cm/ 14-inch cables, as shown in Figure 9.23.

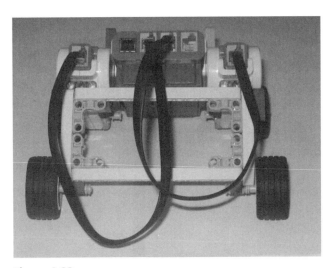

Figure 9.23

Programming Go Bot

Now that Go Bot has been assembled, it is time to begin work on the NXT-G program that will bring it to life. The NXT-G program itself will be relatively simple. It will provide instructions to the Go Bot to perform the following actions:

- Drive forward
- Drive backward
- Spin in place
- Talk
- Display different text messages

The NXT-G program will be created in three distinct stages. In the first stage, the programming blocks needed to control the robot's movement will be added to the program and configured. The robot's operation will then be tested to ensure that things work as they should. Next, Sound and Display blocks will be added to the NXT-G program to give the robot some personality. This will complete the development of the robot's programming. The robot's operations will again be tested. Lastly, you will add comments to the NXT-G program that document its operation, and then you will perform one last test of the robot's operations.

Stage 1—Moving the Robot

Begin the development of Go Bot's NXT-G program by creating a new NXT-G program named Go_Bot. Once created, drag and drop three instances of the Move block onto the program's main sequence beam.

The first Move block will be responsible for moving the robot forward in a straight line. Select it and configure it as follows:

- **Port**—Select ports B and C.
- **Direction**—Select Forward.
- **Steering**—Make sure the slide is centered in the middle of the slider bar, configuring the robot to move forward in a straight line.
- **Power**—Set power to 75 percent.

- **Duration**—Set duration to 5 seconds.
- **Next Action**—Select Brake.

The second Move block will move the robot backward in a straight line to its original starting position. Select it and configure it as follows:

- **Port**—Select ports B and C.
- **Direction**—Select Backward.
- **Steering**—Make sure the slide is centered in the middle of the slider bar, configuring the robot to move backward in a straight line.
- **Power**—Set power to 75 percent.
- **Duration**—Set duration to 5 seconds.
- **Next Action**—Select Brake.

The third Move block will be used to spin the robot full circle, pivoting it along its left front wheel (which is connected to Port C). Select the third Move block and configure it as follows:

- **Port**—Select port C.
- **Direction**—Select Forward.
- **Steering**—N/A.
- **Power**—Set power to 75 percent.
- **Duration**—Set duration to 2900 degrees.
- **Next Action**—Select Brake.

Figure 9.24 shows how the NXT-G program should look at this point. Save the program and then turn on and connect the robot (e.g. NXT Brick) to your computer and download the program by clicking on the NXT Download button located at the bottom right corner of the work area. Once the NXT-G program has been downloaded, disconnect Go Bot and place it on the floor in an area free of obstacles. Press the NXT Brick's orange button four times to select and run the NXT-G program.

Ensure that, once started, the Go Bot moves forward and backward and that it then spins in place. If it does not perform all of these tasks correctly, go back and

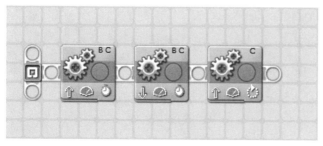

Figure 9.24
A simple starting version of the Go Bot's NXT-G program.

review each of the programming blocks that make up the NXT-G program and ensure that their configuration matches up with the configuration settings specified for each block. Once you have found and corrected any block configuration errors, download and retest Go Bot's operation before proceeding to the second stage of the program's development.

Stage 2—Getting the Robot to Speak and Display Text

Now that Go Bot's base functionality has been programmed and validated, it's time to provide the robot with a little personality through the addition and configuration of Sound, Display, and Wait Sensor programming blocks that together enable the robot to:

- Say "Hello" when first started.
- Display the text string "Hi. I am Go Bot!" on the NXT Brick's LCD.
- Pause for two seconds.
- Play a tone before and after each movement made by Go Bot.
- Say "Goodbye."
- Display the text string "Goodbye" on the NXT Brick's LCD.

Begin by inserting a Sound block on the sequence beam immediately before the first of the three Move blocks. Select the Sound block and configure it as follows:

- **Action**—Select Sound File.
- **Control**—Select Play.
- **Volume**—Set value level to 75 percent.

- **Function**—Ensure that Repeat is not selected.
- **File**—Select Hello from the list of files in the scrolling list box.
- **Wait**—Select Wait for Completion.

Insert a Display block between the Sound block and the first of the three Move blocks. Select the Display block and configure it as follows:

- **Action**—Select Text from the drop-down list.
- **Display**—Select Clear.
- **Text**—Type Hi. I am Go Bot! in the text entry field.
- **Position**—Specify a value of 3 for X and 26 for Y.

Insert a Sensor Wait block in between the Display block and the first of the three Move blocks. Select the Sensor block and configure it as follows:

- **Control**—Select Time from the drop-down list.
- **Until**—Type a value of 2 in the Seconds entry field.

Insert a Sound block between the Sensor Time block and the first of the three Move blocks. Select the Sound block and configure it as follows:

- **Action**—Select Tone.
- **Control**—Select Play.
- **Volume**—Set value level to 75 percent.
- **Function**—Ensure that Repeat is not selected.
- **Note**—Specify a note value of C and set it to play for .5 seconds.
- **Wait**—Select Wait for Completion.

Insert a new Sound block just after the first of the three Move blocks. Select the Sound block and configure it exactly the same way as you did the previous Sound block.

Insert another Sound block just after the second of the three Move blocks. Select the Sound block and configure it exactly the same way as you did the two previous Sound blocks.

Insert another Sound block just after the third of the three Move blocks. Select the Sound block and configure it as follows:

- **Action**—Select Sound File.
- **Control**—Select Play.
- **Volume**—Set value level to 75 percent.
- **Function**—Ensure that Repeat is not selected.
- **File**—Select Goodbye from the list of files in the scrolling list box.
- **Wait**—Select Wait for Completion.

Next, add a Display block to the end of the sequence beam and configure it as follows:

- **Action**—Select Text from the drop-down list.
- **Display**—Select Clear.
- **Text**—Type Goodbye in the text entry field.
- **Position**—Specify a value of 30 for X and 29 for Y.

Lastly, add a Sensor Wait block at the end of the sequence beam. Select the Sensor block and configure it as follows:

- **Control**—Select Time from the drop-down list.
- **Until**—Type a value of 1 in the Seconds entry field.

Figure 9.25 shows how the NXT-G program should now look. Save the program and then turn on and connect the robot (e.g. NXT Brick) to your computer and download the program by clicking on the NXT Download button located at the bottom right corner of the work area. Once the NXT-G program has been downloaded, disconnect Go Bot and place it on the floor in an area free of

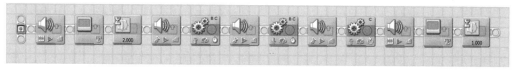

Figure 9.25
This version of the Go_Bot NXT-G program contains all of the robot's programming logic.

obstacles. Press on the NXT Brick's orange button four times to select and run the NXT-G program.

Before continuing to the final stage of the NXT-G program's development, test the robot and make sure it operates as previously described.

Stage 3—Document the NXT-G Program

At this point Go Bot's NXT-G program is almost done. All that remains is for you to document its operation. Update the Go_Bot program so that it contains all of the comments shown in Figure 9.26.

Congratulations on the creation of your very first robot. This is a considerable achievement. Before moving on to Chapter 10, "Tracker Bot," to learn how to further enhance the robot, take a few minutes to fully test the operation of Go Bot, ensuring that it works as described. If it does not perform exactly as has been described, go back and review each of the programming blocks that make up the NXT-G program and ensure that their configuration matches up correctly with the configuration settings that were previously specified for each block.

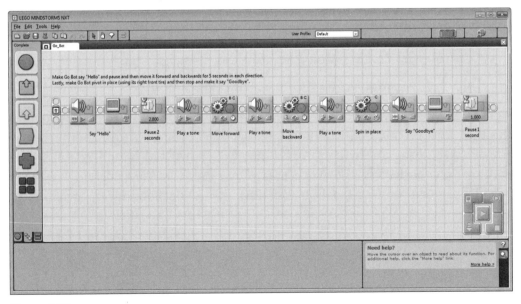

Figure 9.26
The final version of the Go_Bot NXT-G program.

REMOTE CONTROLLING GO BOT

As a moving robot, Go Bot's movement can be controlled via NXT-G programs that you develop and download into the NXT Brick. Alternatively, you can use the Remote Control window to control Go Bot with your mouse or keyboard. To access the Remote Control window, shown in Figure 9.27, click on Tools > Remote Control.

Hint

In order to be able to make effective use of the Remote Control feature, you either need a relatively long USB cable or a wireless Bluetooth connection.

For the remote control to work, the NXT Brick must be powered on and a connection must exist between the robot (e.g. NXT Brick) and your computer. Otherwise, the Remote Control window will appear grayed out and you will not be able to access any of the controls shown on it. Often, Lego Mindstorms NXT 2.0 automatically detects and establishes a connection with the NXT Brick. However, sometimes you may have to do it yourself. To do so, click on the Connections button and then select your NXT Brick and click on the Connections button followed by the Close button.

With a connection established, use your mouse to click on the Forward, Backward, Left, and Right button to remotely control the movement of Go Bot. Alternatively,

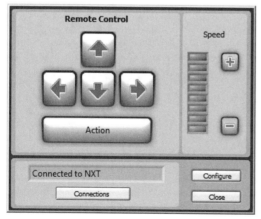

Figure 9.27
Using the Remote Control window to operate Go Bot.

you can use the keyboard's Up, Down, Right, and Left keys to control Go Bot's movement. You can adjust the speed at which Go Bot moves by clicking on either the Increase Speed or Decrease Speed buttons or by clicking directly on the graphic speed meter to indicate the speed at which you want Go Bot to move.

SUMMARY

This chapter showed you how to create your first robotic creation, Go Bot. In developing Go Bot, you learned the fundamental steps involved in robotic development: design, build, program, and test. This chapter explained the importance of breaking down robot development into subassemblies. You also learned how to develop Go Bot's NXT-G program in several stages, testing the robot's operation at the end of each stage. Finally, you learned how to use the Remote Control window to manually take control of Go Bot.

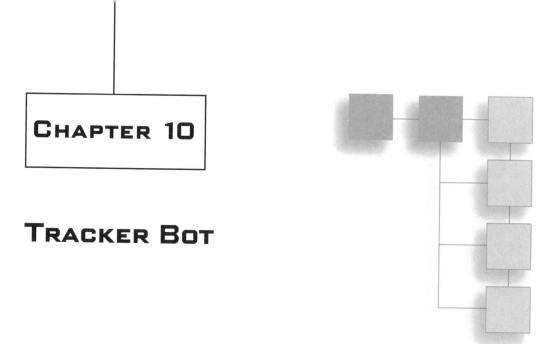

CHAPTER 10

TRACKER BOT

In this chapter, you will learn how to build and program your second robot. This robot, called Tracker Bot, is a modified version of the robot you created in Chapter 9, "Go Bot." Tracker Bot differs from Go Bot in two distinct ways. First, Tracker Bot includes a color sensor that it uses to locate and follow a dark line wherever it may go. Second, Tracker Bot is operated by a totally new NXT-G program, which provides Tracker Bot with the intelligence needed to perform its mission: find and follow the line.

The major topics covered in this chapter include:

- A review of the features and capabilities of Tracker Bot
- Detailed building instructions for Tracker Bot
- Instructions for developing the NXT-G program that operates Tracker Bot

INTRODUCING TRACKER BOT

Tracker Bot's job is to locate and follow a dark line wherever it may go, in a never ending search to go somewhere. Actually "never ending" is a bit of a stretch; in reality, Tracker Bot is controlled by a loop that executes for just 60 seconds before ending. Figure 10.1 provides a sneak peek of Tracker Bot. Note the addition of the color sensor in the front of the robot as well as the additional assembly needed to connect it to the front of the robot.

Figure 10.1
Tracker Bot uses the color sensor in light sensor mode to detect its target path.

Figure 10.2
Go Bot serves as the structural foundation upon which Tracker Bot is built.

BUILDING TRACKER BOT

Tracker Bot is a mobile robot. Since you already have a working mobile robot in the form of Go Bot, shown in Figure 10.2, you can use it as the foundation upon which Tracker Bot is built. Leveraging previous work in this manner is a commonly used design and building technique that Lego Robotic developers take advantage of.

Tracker Bot is created in five steps, outlined here:

- Preparing the color sensor for connection
- Assembling support beams
- Completing the sensor assembly
- Connecting the sensor assembly to the robot
- Programming Tracker Bot

Figure 10.3 provides a complete listing of all the different parts needed to upgrade Go Bot to Tracker Bot. Begin your work on this project by retrieving Go Bot and then getting the pieces pictured in Figure 10.3 from your Lego Mindstorms NXT 2.0 kit.

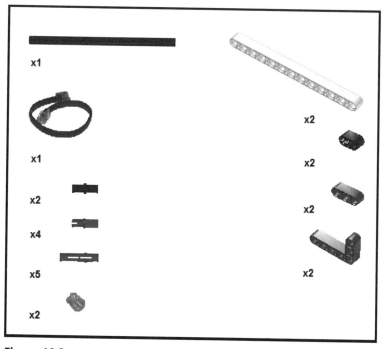

Figure 10.3
The parts inventory list for Tracker Bot.

Preparing the Color Sensor for Connection

Begin the development of Tracker Bot by preparing the color sensor. This involves the attachment of several pegs that will be used to facilitate the connection of the sensor to the robot.

Step 1: Place the color sensor upside down and then connect three connector pegs with friction 3M to it as shown in Figure 10.4.

Figure 10.4

Step 2: Attach two 3M straight beams to the color sensor as shown in Figure 10.5.

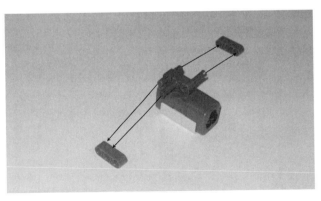

Figure 10.5

Step 3: Take two 2 × 4M perpendicular beams and connect a single connector peg with friction to each. Then connect the 2 × 4M perpendicular beams to the color sensor as shown in Figure 10.6.

Figure 10.6

Hint

Figure 10.7 shows how the color sensor should look now that it has been prepared for connection to the sensor assembly.

Figure 10.7

Assembling Support Beams

The next set of steps involved in the creation of the sensor assembly requires the preparation of additional support beams that will be used to mount the color sensor onto the front of the robot.

Step 1: Take a 13M straight beam and connect a connector peg with friction and cross axle to it and then take a 2M straight beam and connect a connector peg with friction and cross axle and a connector peg with friction 3M to it, as shown in Figure 10.8.

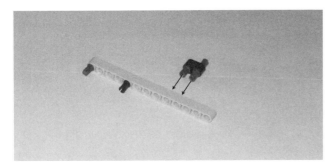

Figure 10.8

Step 2: Connect the two beams used in Step 1 together as shown in Figure 10.9.

Figure 10.9

Step 3: Take another 13M straight beam and connect a connector peg with friction and cross axle to it and then take another 2M straight beam and connect a connector peg with friction and cross axle and a connector peg with friction 3M to it, as shown in Figure 10.10.

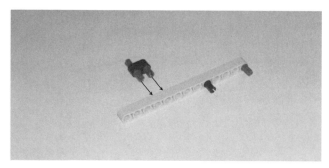

Figure 10.10

Step 4: Connect the two beams used in Step 3 together as shown in Figure 10.11.

Figure 10.11

Completing the Sensor Assembly

Now it is time to finish putting together the sensor assembly. This is accomplished using the color sensor and support beams created in the previous steps.

Step 1: Connect the two sets of support beams to the color sensor, as shown in Figure 10.12.

Figure 10.12

Step 2: The final step in the development of the sensor assembly is to connect a 12M cross axle to the bottom of the assembly, as shown in Figure 10.13.

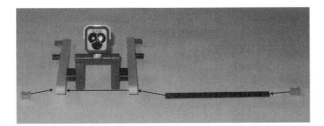

Figure 10.13

Hint

Figure 10.14 shows how the sensor assembly should look once all subcomponents have been connected.

Figure 10.14

Connecting the Sensor Assembly to the Robot

All that is left in the construction of the robot is to attach the sensor assembly to Go Bot, thus creating the Tracker Bot. This connection is facilitated via the beams that protrude from the front of Go Bot.

Step 1: Connect the color sensor assembly to the front of the robot, as shown in Figure 10.15.

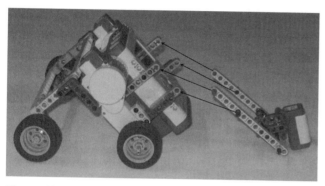

Figure 10.15

Hint

Figure 10.16 shows an example of how Tracker Bot should look once it is fully assembled.

Figure 10.16

Step 2: In order to take advantage of its new sensor assembly attachment, the color sensor must be connected to the NXT Brick. Set this up by connecting the color sensor to the NXT Brick's number 3 port using a 35cm/14-inch cable, as shown in Figure 10.17.

Figure 10.17

Programming Tracker Bot

Now that you have turned Go Bot into Tracker Bot, it is time to develop the NXT-G program that will make use of its new color sensor and turn it into a tracking robot. The NXT-G program itself is relatively straightforward, providing instructions to the Tracker Bot that perform the following actions:

- Repeatedly play a sound file that makes a sonar-type sound
- Briefly pause after playback
- Announce that it is ready to begin tracking
- Use the color sensor in light mode to locate and track a dark-colored line

Tracker Bot's NXT-G program is created in three stages. In the first stage, a loop is set up that contains the programming blocks needed to continually check sensor data and control Tracker Bot's movement. Once this stage is complete, you should put Tracker Bot through its first test run, which you can do using the Mindstorms NXT 2.0 Test Pad that came with your Lego Mindstorms NXT 2.0 kit. Just place the robot on the pad and point it in the direction of the circular black track line that is drawn across the entire pad.

Next, you will add Sound blocks, a Wait block, and a second Loop block to the NXT-G program in order to provide its sound effects. This will complete the development of the robot's programming, allowing you to put it through a second round of testing. The third and final stage of program development consists of documenting the NXT-G program through the addition of comments that explain the program's operation. When done adding the comments, you should, of course, put the robot through one last test of its operation.

Stage 1—Moving the Robot

Begin the development of Tracker Bot's NXT-G program by creating a new NXT-G program named Tracker_Bot. Once created, drag and drop a Loop block onto the main sequence beam. This block will be configured to execute its loop for 60 seconds, at which time Tracker Bot will cease operation. Next, place a Switch block inside the Loop block. The Switch block will be used to configure the color sensor to operate in Light mode and collect and analyze the data that the sensor generates. Finally, drag and drop two Move blocks onto the upper half of the Switch block, and then drag and drop two more Move blocks onto the lower half of the Switch block.

As previously stated, the Loop block will be set up to run for 60 seconds. Select this block and configure it as follows:

- **Control**—Select Time from the drop-down list.
- **Until**—Set Seconds to 60.
- **Show**—Leave the Counter option disabled.

The Switch block must be configured to operate the color sensor in light sensor mode. Select and configure it as follows:

- **Control**—Select Sensor from the drop-down list.
- **Sensor**—Select Color Sensor from the drop-down list.

- **Display**—Leave the Flat view option enabled.
- **Port**—Set the Port assignment to 3.
- **Action**—Select Light Sensor from the drop-down list.
- **Compare**—Specify a value of 40 as the trigger value for the sensor (triggering the sensor whenever a light level above 40% is detected).
- **Function**—Enable the Light option and select the green light (turning on the sensor and enabling it to detect when the light is reflected back to the sensor).

The Switch block collects and analyzes sensor data. The two Move blocks in the upper half of the Switch block are executed when a "light" value (> 40) is detected. The first of these two Move blocks powers the servo motor attached to the NXT Brick B port, moving the robot a little to the left. Select it and configure it as follows:

- **Port**—Select port B.
- **Direction**—Select Forward.
- **Steering**—This option will be disabled.
- **Power**—Set power to 15 percent.
- **Duration**—Select Unlimited.
- **Next Action**—This option will be disabled.

The second Move block in the upper half of the Switch block powers the servo motor attached to the NXT Brick's C port, moving the robot to the right. Select it and configure it as follows:

- **Port**—Select port C.
- **Direction**—Select Forward.
- **Steering**—This option will be disabled.
- **Power**—Set power to 75 percent.
- **Duration**—Select Unlimited.
- **Next Action**—This option will be disabled.

The Move blocks located in the lower half of the Switch block are executed when "dark" value (< 40) is detected. The first of these two Move blocks powers the servo motor attached to the NXT Brick's B port, moving the robot to the left. Select it and configure it as follows:

- **Port**—Select port B.
- **Direction**—Select Forward.
- **Steering**—This option will be disabled.
- **Power**—Set power to 75 percent.
- **Duration**—Select Unlimited.
- **Next Action**—This option will be disabled.

The second Move block in the lower half of the Switch block powers the servo motor attached to the NXT Brick C port, moving the robot a little to the right. Select it and configure it as follows:

- **Port**—Select port C.
- **Direction**—Select Forward.
- **Steering**—This option will be disabled.
- **Power**—Set power to 15 percent.
- **Duration**—Select Unlimited.
- **Next Action**—This option will be disabled.

Figure 10.18 shows how the NXT-G program should look at this point. Save the program. Connect Tracker Bot (e.g. the NXT Brick) to your computer and download the program by clicking on the NXT Download button located at the bottom right corner of the work area. Once the NXT-G program has been downloaded, disconnect Tracker Bot and place it on the Mindstorms NXT 2.0 Test Pad, pointing it in the general direction of the large dark oval drawn on the pad. Press on the NXT Brick's orange button four times to select and run the NXT-G program.

Ensure that Tracker Bot is able to locate and begin following the dark oval line. If Tracker Bot detects and then loses track of the line, restart the program,

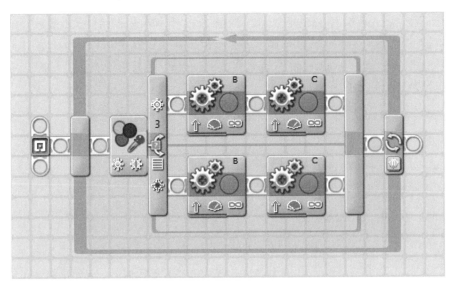

Figure 10.18
This version of the Tracker_Bot program enables the robot's basic execution.

adjusting its starting position, putting it a little more in line with the robot's starting direction. If Tracker Bot does not perform correctly, go back and review each of the programming blocks that make up the NXT-G program and ensure that their configuration matches up with the configuration settings specified for each block and then update, download, and retest the robot again.

Stage 2—Adding Sound Effects

The core functionality needed to make Tracker Bot do its things is now in place. Now it's time to further enhance the NXT-G program, providing the robot with the sound effects needed to make it more interesting to watch and enjoy. This will be accomplished through the addition of a pair of Sound blocks and a Wait block that together enable the Tracker Bot to:

- Play a sonar-like sound at the beginning of its operation
- Pause for two seconds
- Say "OK," announcing that it is ready to begin tracking

Begin by inserting a Loop block on the sequence beam immediately before the Loop block. Configure it to repeat its execution three times by selecting it and configuring it as follows:

- **Control**—Select Count from the drop-down list.
- **Until**—Set Count to 3.
- **Show**—Leave the Counter option disabled.

Drag and drop a Sound block inside the Loop blocks that you just configured. Select the Sound block and configure it as follows:

- **Action**—Select Sound File.
- **Control**—Select Play.
- **Volume**—Set value level to 75 percent.
- **Function**—Ensure that Repeat is not selected.
- **File**—Select !Sonar from the list of files in the scrolling list box.
- **Wait**—Select Wait for Completion.

Hint

Sound files with the ! character as the first character in their file name are played sound effects. All other sound files represent spoken words.

Tracker Bot will now begin its execution after playing a sonar sound three times. Next, add a Sensor Wait block to the main sequence beam, placing it between the NXT-G program's two loops. Select the Wait block and configure it as follows.

- **Control**—Select Time from the drop-down list.
- **Until**—Type a value of 2 in the Seconds entry field.

Next, add a final Sound block to the NXT-G program, placing it immediately before the second Loop block. Select the Sound block and configure it as follows.

- **Action**—Select Sound File.
- **Control**—Select Play.

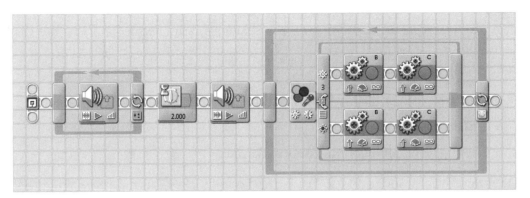

Figure 10.19
A more robust version of the Tracker Bot program.

- **Volume**—Set value level to 75 percent.
- **Function**—Ensure that Repeat is not selected.
- **File**—Select OK from the list of files in the scrolling list box.
- **Wait**—Select Wait for Completion.

Figure 10.19 shows how the Tracker_Bot program should now look. If you have not done so, go ahead and save the program, connect the robot (e.g. the NXT Brick) to your computer and download the program by clicking on the NXT Download button located at the bottom right corner of the work area. Disconnect Tracker Bot, place it on the Mindstorms NXT 2.0 Test Pad and press on the NXT Brick's orange button four times to select and run the NXT-G program.

Before continuing to the final stage of the NXT-G Program's development, test the robot and make sure it operates as previously described.

Stage 3—Documenting the NXT-G Program

At this point, Tracker Bot's NXT-G program is almost done. What remains is to document its operation. This is accomplished by adding the comments shown in Figure 10.20 to the program.

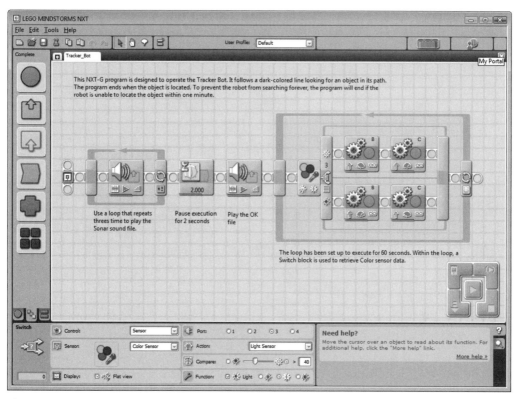

Figure 10.20
The final version of the Tracker_Bot NXT-G program.

Congratulations on the completion of another robot development project. Before moving on to Chapter 11, "Detector Bot," take a few minutes to fully test Tracker Bot. Make sure everything works as has been described. If necessary, go back and review each of the programming blocks that make up the NXT-G program and check to see if you made any configuration errors.

SUMMARY

This chapter took you step-by-step through the steps required to modify and enhance Go Bot and turn it into Tracker Bot. In doing so, you gained practical experience working with the color sensor. You also got the chance to stretch your NXT-G programming skills, employing conditional logic and a loop, as you wrote the program file that tied everything together.

CHAPTER 11

DETECTOR BOT

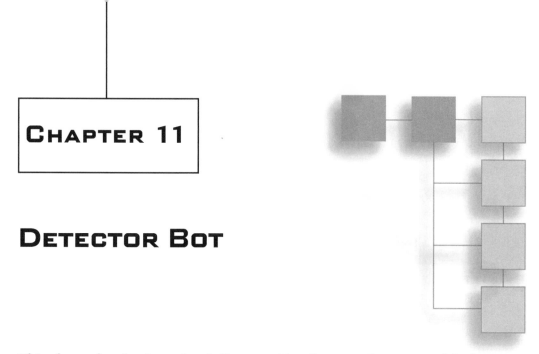

This chapter's robotic project is Detector Bot. Detector Bot is a modified version of Tracker Bot. Its job is to seek out an object located at the end of its path. It features a new assembly that includes a touch sensor. This allows the robot to detect when it comes into contact with its target object. With this new sensor assembly in place, the robot will be able to finally reach the end of its quest, following its path until it finds its objective.

The major topics covered in this chapter include:

- A review of the features and capabilities of Detector Bot
- Detailed building instructions for Detector Bot
- Instructions for developing the NXT-G program that operates Detector Bot

INTRODUCING DETECTOR BOT

Detector Bot represents another evolutionary step in the development of the robot that you developed in Chapter 9, "Go Bot." In this chapter, the robot is enhanced with a touch sensor, enabling it to detect when it comes into contact with another object. Along with this new capability comes a new job for Detector Bot: to follow its assigned path until it finds its target object, which can be a book, a shoe, or anything else you choose to place in the robot's path.

Figure 11.1
Detector Bot uses a touch sensor to determine when it has found its target.

Figure 11.1 shows how Detector Bot will look when it is complete. Note the addition of the touch sensor located in the front of the robot as well as the use of a cross axle and two teeth that extend the ability of the touch sensor to detect objects along a wider path.

Building Detector Bot

Tracker Bot, shown in Figure 11.2, is the starting point for the creation of Detector Bot. Detector Bot has a new touch sensor assembly that allows it to determine when it comes into contact with other objects.

Figure 11.2
Tracker Bot will serve as the basis for building Detector Bot.

Detector Bot will be created in six steps, as outlined here:

- Preparing the touch sensor for connection
- Connecting screens to the assembly
- Adding support beams to the assembly
- Extending touch sensor reach
- Connecting the touch sensor assembly
- Programming Detector Bot

Figure 11.3 provides a complete inventory of the parts needed to enhance Tracker Bot and turn it into Detector Bot. Begin your work on this project by retrieving these parts from your Lego Mindstorms NXT 2.0 kit.

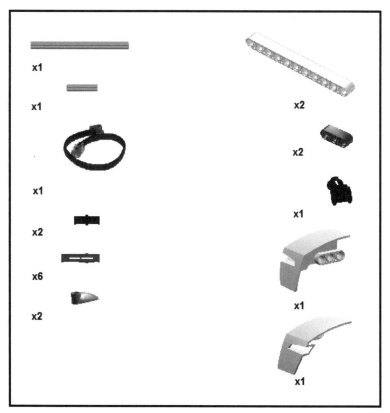

Figure 11.3
The parts inventory list for Detector Bot.

Preparing the Touch Sensor for Connection

Begin the development of Detector Bot by preparing the touch sensor for connection to the robot. This involves the connection of several connector pegs with friction 3M and a pair of 3M straight beams to the sensor.

Step 1: Place the touch sensor upside down and connect a connector peg with friction 3M to it, as shown in Figure 11.4.

Figure 11.4

Step 2: Attach two connector pegs with friction 3M to two 3M straight beams, as shown in Figure 11.5.

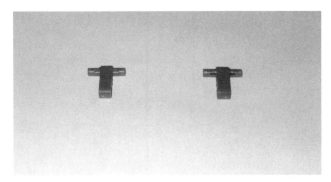

Figure 11.5

Step 3: Take the two 3M straight beams and connect them to the touch sensor using the already attached connector pegs with friction 3M, as shown in Figure 11.6.

Figure 11.6

Hint

Figure 11.7 shows how the touch sensor looks now that it has been prepared for connection to the sensor assembly.

Figure 11.7

Connecting Screens to the Assembly

To give Detector Bot a bit of an armored look and feel, let's connect the left and right screens to the touch sensor, providing the sensor with a little added protection in the process. In addition to making the touch sensor assembly look a little snazzier, these screens also assist with the sensor's connection to the robot and serve as key components to connect the sensor to its support beams.

Step 1: Place the left and right screens upside down on a flat surface and connect a connector peg with friction and a connector peg with friction 3M to each screen, as shown in Figure 11.8.

Figure 11.8

Step 2: Place the touch sensor in an upright position between the two screens and connect the screens to the sensor, as shown in Figure 11.9.

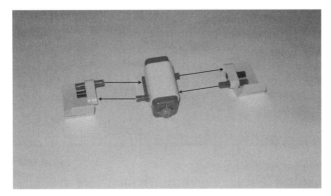

Figure 11.9

Hint

Figure 11.10 shows how the touch sensor looks now that it has been connected to the left screen and the right screen.

Figure 11.10

Adding Support Beams to the Assembly

In order to connect the touch sensor to the robot, you need to provide the assembly with a pair of support beams.

Step 1: Connect a pair of connector pegs with friction 3M to two 11M straight beams, as shown in Figure 11.11.

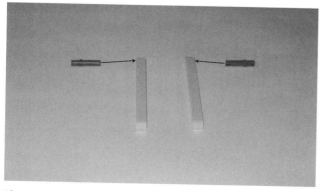

Figure 11.11

Step 2: Connect the support beams to the touch sensor assembly, as shown in Figure 11.12.

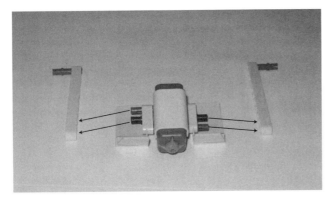

Figure 11.12

Figure 11.13 shows how the touch sensor assembly looks now that its support beams have been added.

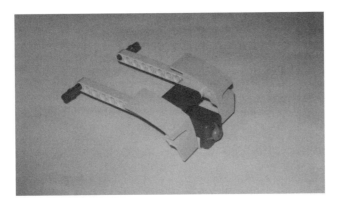

Figure 11.13

Extending Touch Sensor Reach

The touch sensor is able to detect contact with another object only along a very small area (its orange tip). It is possible for the robot to come into contact with another object but for the touch sensor not to detect it unless the object is placed dead center in front of the robot. By adding a small attachment to the front of the touch sensor, you can significantly expand its reach.

Step 1: Insert a 9M cross axle into a catch with cross hole and then center the catch on the axle. Add a pair of teeth to the end of the 9M cross axle and connect a 3M cross axle to the open end of the catch with cross hole, as shown in Figure 11.14.

Figure 11.14

Step 2: Connect the component you assembled in the previous step to the touch sensor assembly, as shown in Figure 11.15.

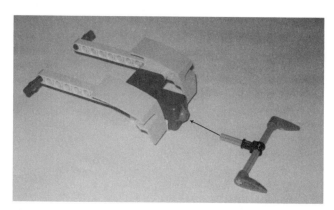

Figure 11.15

Hint

Figure 11.16 shows how the touch sensor assembly looks now that it has been completely assembled.

Figure 11.16

Connecting the Touch Sensor Assembly

Now that the touch sensor assembly has been fully assembled, it can be connected to the robot.

Step 1: Withdraw the two connector pegs with friction 3M from the end of both 11M straight beams and slide the beams between the robot's color sensor and the support beams to which the color sensor is attached. Attach the end of the touch sensor assembly's support beams to the robot, as shown in Figure 11.17 using the two connector pegs with friction 3M that you previously withdrew.

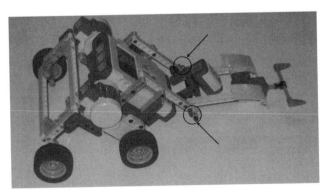

Figure 11.17

Hint

When properly attached, the touch sensor can be raised or lowered. When lowered, it should float approximately a quarter inch above the surface of the ground.

Step 2: Using a 20cm/8-inch cable, connect the touch sensor to Port 1 on the NXT Brick, as shown in Figure 11.18.

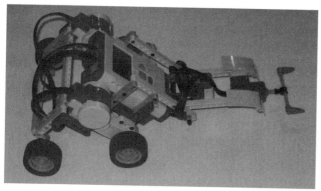

Figure 11.18

Programming Detector Bot

Now that you have completed the transformation of Tracker Bot into Detector Bot, it is time to update the robot's NXT-G program, enabling it to capture and process touch sensor input. The NXT-G program enhancements include the expansion of the NXT-G program's loop in order to incorporate the continuous collection and analysis of touch sensor input. Specifically, the program will be modified to accommodate the following actions:

- Repeatedly collect and analyze touch sensor data.

- Announce that an object has been detected and display a corresponding message on the NXT Brick's LCD when the robot makes contact with another object.

- Halt program and robot execution when contact is made with another object.

■ Play a Game Over message and display corresponding text if the robot does not make contact with another object within 60 seconds.

As with previous projects, Detector Bot's NXT-G program will be developed in a series of stages. In the first stage, Tracker Bot's program will be copied and renamed. In the second stage, the program's programming logic will be updated to include the collection and analysis of touch sensor input and to halt program execution if appropriate. Once this stage is complete, you will put Detector Bot through its first test run to ensure that the program enhancements work correctly.

In the third stage of the NXT-G program's development, you will add programming logic that announces the end of the program's execution (when 60 seconds has expired without the robot detecting its target object). You will once again test the robot's operation, this time to validate that the program shuts down the robot's execution, as just described, when time expires. The fourth and final stage of the NXT-G program's development enhances the program through the addition of comments.

Stage 1—Creating a NXT-G Program for Detector Bot

Stage 1 of the development of the NXT-G program for Detector Bot is quite simple. Begin by making a copy of the Tracker_Bot program, renaming it Detect_Bot. Double click on the Detect_Bot program to open and load it into Lego Mindstorms NXT 2.0 GUI. Verify that it contains the programming logic outlined in Figure 11.19.

Stage 2—Incorporating and Analyzing Touch Sensor Data

Stage 2 involves the incorporation of programming logic that captures and analyzes touch sensor data and manages early program termination when the robot detects contact with another object in its path.

Begin by dragging and dropping a Switch code block inside the program's Loop block, placing it after the existing Switch block (which processes color sensor data). Select and configure the new Switch block as follows:

■ **Control**—Select Sensor from the drop-down list.

■ **Sensor**—Select Touch Sensor from the drop-down list.

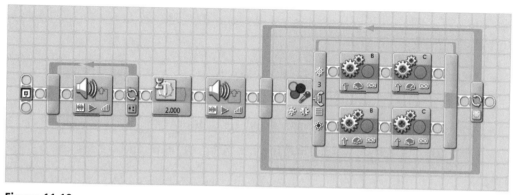

Figure 11.19
Tracker Bot's NXT_G program serves as the starting point in the development of the Detector Bot's program.

- **Display**—Make sure the Flat View option is selected.
- **Port**—Select port 1.
- **Action**—Select Pressed as the action that will trigger the program blocks located in the upper half of the Switch block.

Next add a sound block to the upper half of the Switch block. This block will be used to play an audio file when the robot makes contact with another object. Select and configure the new Sound block as follows:

- **Action**—Select Sound File.
- **Control**—Select Play.
- **Volume**—Set value level to 100 percent.
- **Function**—Ensure that Repeat is not selected.
- **File**—Select Object Detected from the list of files in the scrolling list box.
- **Wait**—Select Wait for Completion.

A message should be displayed on the NXT Brick's LCD announcing when an object has been detected. To do so, drag and drop a Display block onto the top half of the Switch block, placing it after the Sound block. Select the Display block and configure it as follows.

- **Action**—Select Text from the drop-down list.
- **Display**—Select Clear.
- **Text**—Type Object found in the text field entry box.
- **Position**—Specify a value of 8 for the X coordinate and 32 for the Y coordinate.

Drag and drop a Sensor Wait block at the end of the sequence beam. Select the Sensor block and configure it as follows:

- **Control**—Select Time from the drop-down list.
- **Until**—Type a value of 1 in the Seconds entry field.

Next, drag and drop a Stop block into the Switch block, placing it after the Display block. The Stop block has no configuration panel. Its purpose is to halt the execution of the NXT-G program.

Figure 11.20 shows how the programming logic outlined in the program's loop should look at this point in the NXT-G program's development.

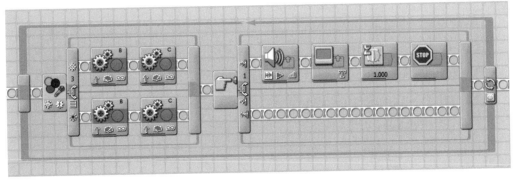

Figure 11.20
The programming logic in the NXT-G program's loop has been enhanced to capture touch sensor data and to control early program termination.

Before continuing to the final stage of the NXT-G program's development, set aside some time to test the robot and make sure it operates as previously described. Start by saving the program. Next, connect the robot (e.g., the NXT Brick) to your computer and download the program by clicking on the NXT Download button located at the bottom right corner of the work area. Disconnect Tracker Bot, place it on the Mindstorms NXT 2.0 Test Pad and press on the NXT Brick's orange button four times to select and run the NXT-G program. Once you have verified that the robot has successfully located and begun tracking the path outlined by the solid block line, place an object like a book or soda can in Detector Bot's path and make sure the robot detects the object and then halts.

If Detector Bot does not perform as expected, go back and review each of the programming blocks that you added to the new Switch block that you inserted inside the program Loop block and ensure that their configuration matches up with the configuration settings specified for each block. If you find any errors in block configuration, correct the errors and then download, and retest the robot again.

Stage 3—Enhancing Program Termination

The last stage in the development of Detector Bot's NXT-G program requires the addition of two programming blocks. These blocks will not materially affect the operation of the robot. Their purpose is to shut down the robot after 60 seconds of operation.

Begin by dragging and dropping a Sound block to the end of the sequence beam, just after the end of the program's Loop block. Select the Sound block and configure it as follows.

- **Action**—Select Sound File.
- **Control**—Select Play.
- **Volume**—Set value level to 75 percent.
- **Function**—Ensure that Repeat is not selected.
- **File**—Select Game Over from the list of files in the scrolling list box.
- **Wait**—Select Wait for Completion.

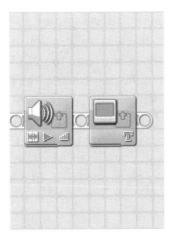

Figure 11.21
If 60 seconds pass with no collision, the NXT-G stops its execution and announces that it has failed to locate its target.

Wrap things up by dragging and dropping a Display block onto the end of the sequence beam, placing it just after the Sound block that you just configured. Select the Display block and configure it as follows.

- **Action**—Select Text from the drop-down list.
- **Display**—Select Clear.
- **Text**—Type Object not found in the text field entry box.
- **Position**—Specify a value of 3 for the X coordinate and 28 for the Y coordinate.

At this point, you have completed the development of the NXT-G program's programming logic. Figure 11.21 shows how the two programming blocks that you just added should look.

Stage 4—Documenting Your NXT_G Program

All that remains to wrap up your work on Detector Bot is to update the NXT program's internal documentation through the addition of comments that explain the program's purpose and operation. This is accomplished by adding the comments shown in Figure 11.22 to the program.

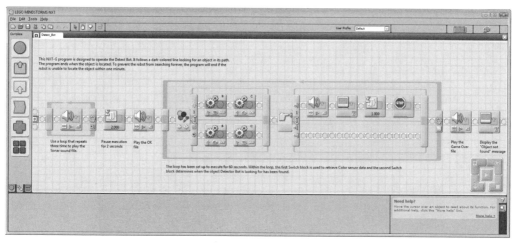

Figure 11.22
The final version of the Detect_Bot NXT-G program.

Summary

In this chapter you learned how to enhance Tracker Bot, turning it into Detector Bot through the addition of a new touch sensor assembly and the extension of its NXT-G program. Detector Bot sill locates and follows a dark line wherever it may go. However, the robot now has the ability to determine when it comes into contact with another object, allowing it to ascertain when it has found its target object and completed its mission.

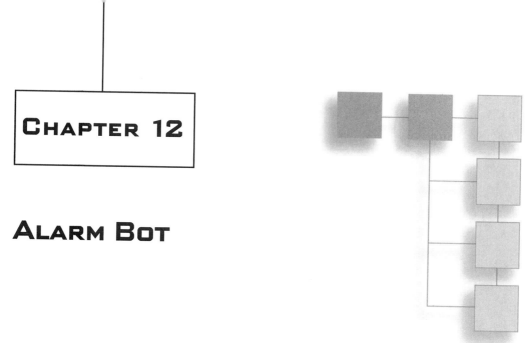

CHAPTER 12

ALARM BOT

Congratulations on making it to the final chapter in this book. In this chapter you will complete one last robot development project, creating a new robot named Alarm Bot. Alarm Bot is an automation guard robot that generates an alert whenever it detects an object within four feet of the robot in any direction. This is accomplished using the ultrasonic sensor, which is repeatedly spun around in a 360-degree circle, allowing the robot to track intruders approaching from any possible direction.

The major topics covered in this chapter include:

- A review of the features and capabilities of Alarm Bot
- Detailed building instructions for Alarm Bot
- Instructions for developing the NXT-G program that operates Alarm Bot

INTRODUCING ALARM BOT

Alarm Bot's job is to detect and generate an alarm whenever it detects an object within its range of operation. Figure 12.1 provides a sneak peek of Alarm Bot. Note that in addition to using the ultrasonic sensor to detect intruders, Alarm Bot also has a color sensor, which it operates as a multi-colored lamp, flashing different colors and playing alarm messages whenever it sounds an alarm.

Alarm Bot is designed to be placed in the center of any room and to generate an audio alarm if it detects any object (intruder) within a four-foot radius. Figure 12.2

Figure 12.1
Alarm Bot's electronic components consist of two sensors and a servo motor.

provides a graphical representation of Alarm Bot's radius of detection. Alarm Bot's radius consists of a full 360-degree circle that extends four feet out from the robot's location.

Building Alarm Bot

Alarm Bot consists of a wide collection of electronic and nonelectronic components. To simplify its construction, it will be created in a series of eight steps, as outlined here:

- Assembling a framework base
- Adding a platform to the NXT Brick to support the servo motor
- Adding support struts to support the servo motor
- Connecting the servo motor
- Preparing the ultrasonic sensor

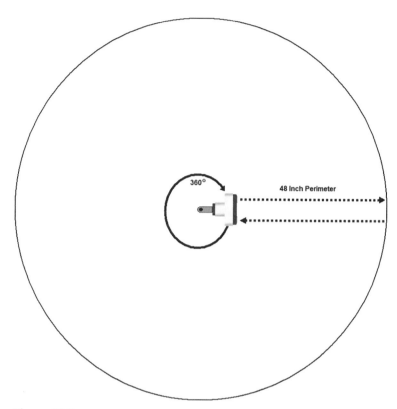

Figure 12.2
Alarm Bot uses the ultrasonic sensor to detect when an object comes within 48 inches of the robot.

- Preparing the color sensor
- Completing Alarm Bot's assembly
- Programming Alarm Bot

Figure 12.3 provides a complete inventory of the parts needed to build Alarm Bot. Begin your work on this project by retrieving these parts from your Lego Mindstorms NXT 2.0 kit.

Assembling a Framework Base

Begin the development of Alarm Bot by preparing a base framework to which the NXT Brick can be attached and that will serve as the foundation upon which the robot is built.

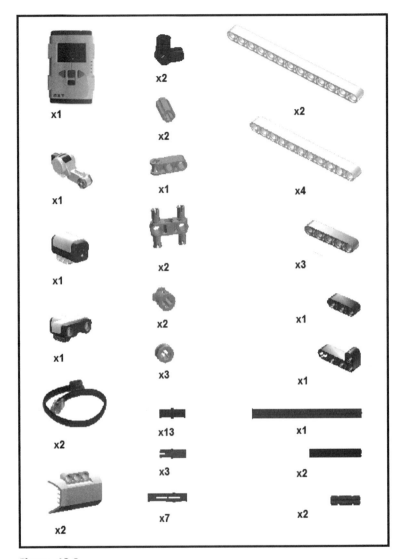

Figure 12.3
The parts inventory list for Alarm Bot.

Step 1: Attach two 11M straight beams to the right side of the NXT Brick using four connector pegs with friction.

Step 2: Connect the lower end of the two 11M straight beams to a 13M straight beam using two more connector pegs with friction.

Step 3: Connect one additional connector peg with friction directly to the NXT Brick, as shown in Figure 12.4.

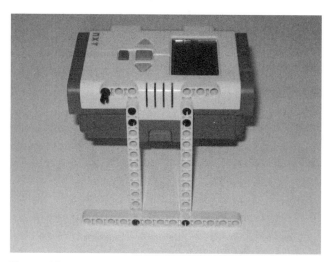

Figure 12.4

Step 4: Attach two more 11M straight beams to the left side of the NXT Brick using four connector pegs with friction.

Step 5: Connect the lower end of the two 11M straight beams to a 13M straight beam using two more connector pegs with friction, as shown in Figure 12.5.

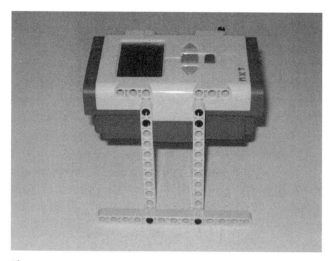

Figure 12.5

Adding a Platform to the NXT Brick to Support the Servo Motor

Now it's time to modify the base framework by adding a platform that will be used to support the addition of the robot's servo motor.

Step 1: Connect two 3M pegged blocks together, as shown in Figure 12.6.

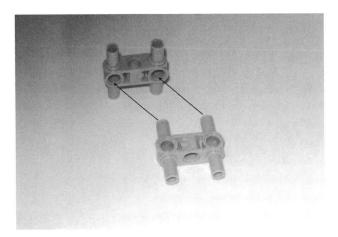

Figure 12.6

Step 2: Connect three 5M straight beams together using a pair of 3M connector pegs with friction, as shown in Figure 12.7.

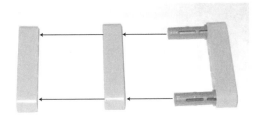

Figure 12.7

Step 3: Connect the pair of 3M pegged blocks to the three 5M straight beams, as shown in Figure 12.8.

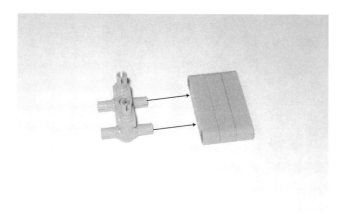

Figure 12.8

Hint

Figure 12.9 shows how the support platform looks once it is assembled.

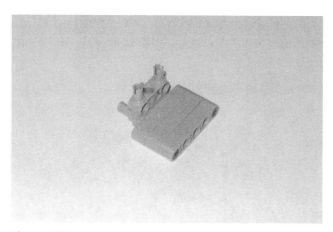

Figure 12.9

Step 4: Connect the support platform to the framework base, as shown in Figure 12.10.

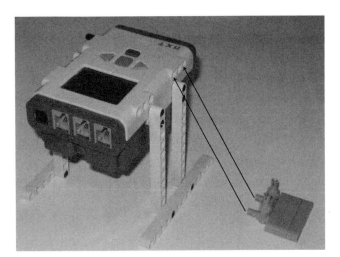

Figure 12.10

Adding Support Struts to Support the Servo Motor

In addition to the support platform, the robot's servo motor will also be supported by a pair of support struts, which help to keep the servo motor firmly in place.

Step 1: Connect a connector peg with friction, a cross axle extension, a 2M cross axle with grooves, an angle connector 90 degrees, a 4M cross axle and a bushing together, as shown in Figure 12.11.

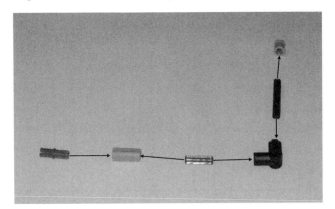

Figure 12.11

Step 2: Assemble a second support strut.

Step 3: Connect both sets of support struts to the framework base, as shown in Figure 12.12.

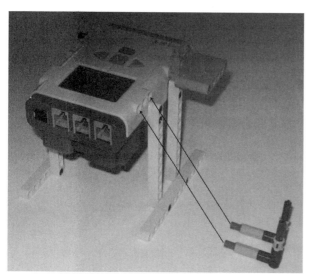

Figure 12.12

Hint

Figure 12.13 shows how the support struts look after they are added to the framework base.

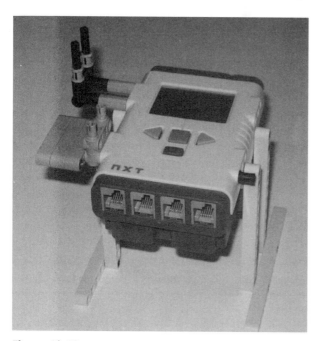

Figure 12.13

Connecting the Servo Motor

Now it is time to connect the servo motor to the robot. The servo motor will be used to rotate the robot's ultrasonic sensor left, and then right, a full 360 degrees each time.

Step 1: Attach the servo motor to the 3M pegged block that makes up part of the support platform, as shown in Figure 12.14.

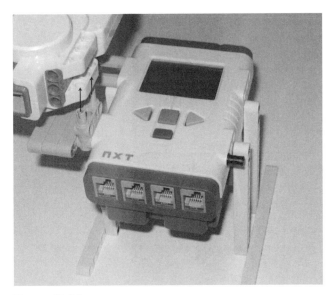

Figure 12.14

Step 2: As you attach the servo motor to the 3M pegged block, make sure you also connect the servo motor to the two support struts, as shown in Figure 12.15.

Hint

Figure 12.16 shows how the robot should look now that the servo motor has been attached.

Figure 12.15

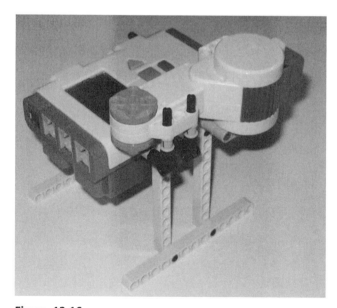

Figure 12.16

Step 3: Finish securing the servo motor to the robot by capping the two 4M cross axles at the top of the support struts with two half-bushings, as shown in Figure 12.17.

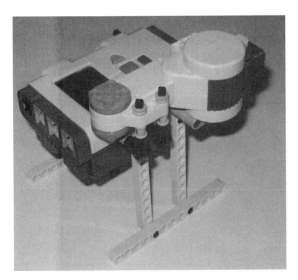

Figure 12.17

Preparing the Ultrasonic Sensor

At this point, the framework for Alarm Bot is complete. All that remains is to assemble and connect its sensor subassemblies. The first of these assemblies is the ultrasonic sensor subassembly.

Step 1: Take two 5M straight beams, two 3M connector pegs with friction, a 3M cross block, and the ultrasonic sensor and connect them, as shown in Figure 12.18.

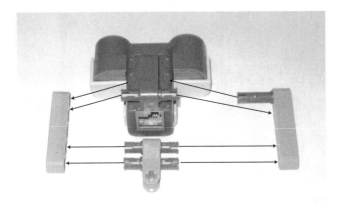

Figure 12.18

Step 2: Place the ultrasonic sensor on its side, push an 8M cross axle with end stop all the way through the 3M cross block, and then lock the 8M cross axle with end stop into place using a half-bushing, as shown in Figure 12.19.

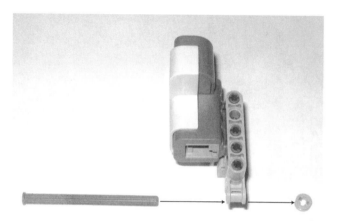

Figure 12.19

Step 3: Attach a connector peg with friction to each of the two design shells, as shown in Figure 12.20, and then use the connector pegs with friction to connect the two design shells to the ultrasonic sensor.

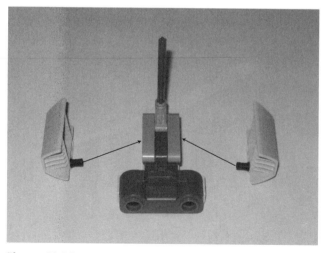

Figure 12.20

Step 4: Connect the ultrasonic sensor subassembly to the robot by inserting the open end of the 8M cross axle with end stop into the crosshair connection located in the center of the servo motor's upper side, as shown in Figure 12.21.

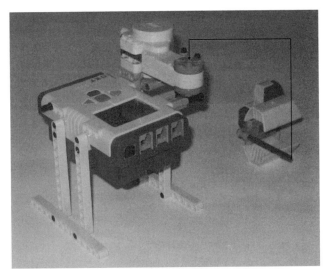

Figure 12.21

Preparing the Color Sensor

Alarm Bot's color sensor subassembly is the last component required to finish building the robot.

Step 1: Connect a connector peg with friction and a 3M connector peg with friction and a cross axle to the 2 × 4 perpendicular beam, and then connect the 3M straight beam to a 3M connector peg with friction, as shown in Figure 12.22.

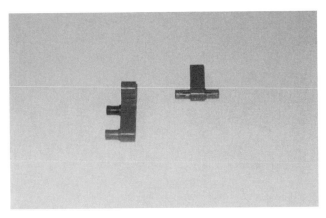

Figure 12.22

Step 2: Connect the 2×4 perpendicular beam to the 3M straight beam by inserting one end of the 3M Connector Peg into the hole located in the foot of the 2×4 Perpendicular beam, and then connect the resulting component to the color sensor, as shown in Figure 12.23.

Figure 12.23

Step 3: Connect the color sensor subassembly to the robot, as shown in Figure 12.24.

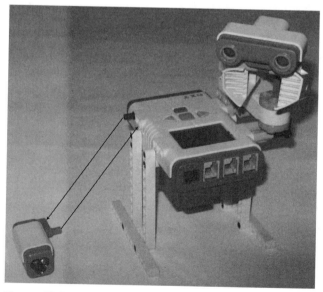

Figure 12.24

Hint

Figure 12.25 shows how Alarm Bot looks after it is fully assembled.

Figure 12.25

Completing Alarm Bot's Assembly

Now that Alarm Bot is completely assembled, all that remains is to connect the servo motor and the sensors to the NXT Brick. To do so, take a 35 cm/14-inch cable and attach one end of it to the ultrasonic sensor and the other end to the number 4 port on the NXT Brick. Next, take another 35 cm/14-inch cable and use it to connect the color sensor to the number 3 port on the NXT Brick. Lastly, use another 35 cm/14-inch cable to connect the servo motor to the NXT Brick's A port. See Figure 12.26.

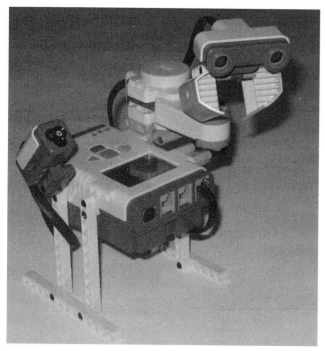

Figure 12.26

Programming Alarm Bot

Now that you have finished the construction of Alarm Bot, it's time to begin work on the NXT-G program that controls its operation. This program is made up of program blocks located on two separate sequence beams, both of which are controlled by loops. The program blocks on the first sequence beam control the operation of the ultrasonic sensor, collecting and analyzing its input and generating an alarm if an intruder is detected. The program blocks on the second sequence beam control the operation of the robot's servo motor, making it rotate the ultrasonic sensor 360 degrees forward and then 360 degrees backward, over and over again.

As has been the case with all previous robotic development projects, Alarm Bot's NXT-G program will be developed in a series of stages. In the first stage, the program logic that manages the collection and analysis of ultrasonic data is created. In the second stage, the program logic that controls the operation of the servo motor is developed. The third stage of the NXT-G program's development involves the addition of comments that document the NXT-G program and its operation.

Stage 1—Programming the Operation of the Ultrasonic Sensor

As previously stated, the first stage in the development of the NXT-G program involves the operation of the ultrasonic sensor. All programming logic development in this state is done on the program's main sequence beam. Begin by creating a new NXT-G program called Alarm_Bot.

Begin program development by dragging and dropping a Color Lamp block onto the main sequence beam. Select and configure the block as follows:

- **Port**—Select the number 3 port.
- **Action**—Disable the display of light on the color sensor by selecting the Off option.
- **Color**—Leave the default Red color selected.

Next, drag and drop a Loop block onto the main sequence beam, placing it after the Color Lamp block. Select the Loop block and configure it as follows:

- **Control**—Create an endless loop by selecting the Forever option from the drop-down list.
- **Show**—Leave the Counter option unselected.

Add an instance of the Switch Sensor block inside the Loop block. Select the Switch block and configure it as follows:

- **Control**—Select Sensor from the drop-down list.
- **Sensor**—Select Ultrasonic Sensor from the drop-down list.
- **Display**—Leave the default Flat view option enabled.
- **Port**—Select the number 4 port.
- **Compare**—Set the distance option to less than 48 inches.
- **Show**—Select Inches from the drop-down list.

Add a second loop to the main sequence beam, placing it within the upper half of the Switch block. Programming blocks in the upper half of the Switch block execute whenever the robot detects an intruder. Select it and configure it as follows:

- **Control**—Select Count from the drop-down list.
- **Until**—Configure the loop to repeat two times every time it is executed by typing a value of 2 in the Count entry field.
- **Show**—Leave the Counter option unselected.

Drag and drop another Color Lamp block onto the main sequence beam, placing it with the loop located in the upper half of the Switch block. Select and configure the Color Lamp block as follows:

- **Port**—Select the number 3 port.
- **Action**—Turn on the sensor lamp by selecting the On option.
- **Color**—Select the green lamp color.

Drag and drop a second Color Lamp block into the upper half of the Switch block. Select and configure the Color Lamp block as follows:

- **Port**—Select the number 3 port.
- **Action**—Turn on the sensor lamp by selecting the On option.
- **Color**—Select the blue lamp color.

Drag and drop a third Color Lamp block into the upper half of the Switch block. Select and configure the Color Lamp block as follows:

- **Port**—Select the number 3 port.
- **Action**—Turn on the sensor lamp by selecting the On option.
- **Color**—Select the red lamp color.

Drag a Sound block into the upper half of the Switch block. Select and configure the Sound block as follows:

- **Action**—Select Sound File.

- **Control**—Select Play.

- **Volume**—Set value level to 100 percent.

- **Function**—Ensure that Repeat is not selected.

- **File**—Select Alarm from the list of files in the scrolling list box.

- **Wait**—Select Wait for Completion.

Drag another Sound block into the upper half of the Switch block. Select and configure the Sound block as follows:

- **Action**—Select Sound File.

- **Control**—Select Play.

- **Volume**—Set value level to 100 percent.

- **Function**—Ensure that Repeat is not selected.

- **File**—Select Object Detected from the list of files in the scrolling list box.

- **Wait**—Select Wait for Completion.

Finally, drag and drop one more Color Lamp block onto the bottom half of the Switch block. This block executes when the robot does not detect an intruder. Select the Color Lamp block and configure it as follows:

- **Port**—Select the number 3 port.

- **Action**—Turn on the sensor lamp by selecting the Off option.

- **Color**—Select the red lamp color.

Figure 12.27 shows how the programming logic outlined in the program's loop should look at this point in the NXT-G program's development.

Before moving on to the next stage of the NXT-G program's development, take a little time to test the robot and make sure that when the NXT-G program runs its ultrasonic sensor operates properly. Start by saving the program. Next, connect the robot (e.g., the NXT Brick) to your computer and download the program by clicking on the NXT Download button located at the bottom right corner of the work area. Disconnect Alarm Bot, place it in the center of the room with no other obstacles within 48 inches of the direction that the ultrasonic sensor is pointing. Press the NXT Brick's orange button four times to select and

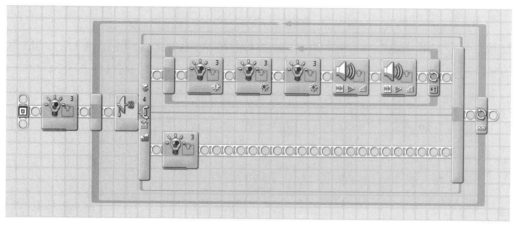

Figure 12.27
These programming blocks manage the operation of the robot's ultrasonic sensor.

run the NXT-G program. Nothing should happen. Next, move within 48 inches of the front of the ultrasonic sensor. It should detect you and signal the alarm. Move out of range of the ultrasonic sensor and the alarm should stop sounding.

If Alarm Bot does not perform as expected, go back and review each of the programming blocks that you added to the program and ensure that their configuration matches up with the configuration settings specified for each block. If you find any errors in block configuration, correct the errors and then download and retest the robot again.

Stage 2—Programming the Operation of the Ultrasonic Sensor

Stage 2 of the development of the Alarm_Bot program involves the incorporation of programming logic that repeatedly rotates the ultrasonic sensor, allowing it to detect intruders within a full 360-degree radius of the robot.

Begin by extending the NXT-G program's lower sequence beam down three inches and then drawing it to the right two more inches. Next, drag and drop a Loop code block onto the lower sequence beam. Select and configure the Loop block as follows:

- **Control**—Create an endless loop by selecting the Forever option from the drop-down list.

- **Show**—Leave the Counter option unselected.

Next, drag and drop a Motor block onto the lower sequence beam's Loop block. Select the Motor block and configure it as follows:

- **Port**—Select the A port.
- **Direction**—Set direction to Forward.
- **Action**—Select Constant from the drop-down list.
- **Power**—Set the power level to 20.
- **Control**—Leave the Motor Power option disabled.
- **Duration**—Set duration to 360 degrees.
- **Wait**—Make sure the Wait for Completion option is selected.
- **Next Action**—Select the Brake option.

Lastly, drag and drop a second Motor block onto the lower sequence beam's Loop block. Select the Motor block and configure it as follows:

- **Port**—Select the A port.
- **Direction**—Set direction to Backward.
- **Action**—Select Constant from the drop-down list.
- **Power**—Set the power level to 20.
- **Control**—Leave the Motor Power option disabled.
- **Duration**—Set duration to 360 degrees.
- **Wait**—Make sure the Wait for Completion option is selected.
- **Next Action**—Select the Brake option.

At this point, you have completed the development of the NXT-G program's programming logic. Figure 12.28 shows how the program should now look.

It's a good idea to test the updates you just made to the NXT-G program before moving on to the last stage of the NXT-G program's development. To do so, start the program and connect the robot (e.g., the NXT Brick) to your computer and download the program by clicking on the NXT Download button located at the bottom right corner of the work area.

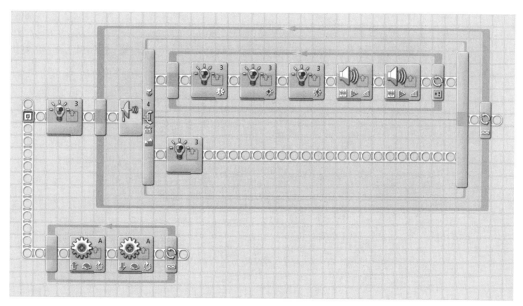

Figure 12.28
The Alarm_Bot program now uses the sensor motor to rotate the ultrasonic sensor.

Next, disconnect Alarm Bot and place it in the center of the room with no other obstacles within 48 inches of the direction that the ultrasonic sensor is pointing. Press the NXT Brick's orange button four times to select and run the NXT-G program. Nothing should happen. However, when you move within 48 inches of the front of the ultrasonic sensor from any direction, it should detect you and signal the alarm, and when you move out of range of the ultrasonic sensor, the alarm should stop sounding.

Stage 3—Documenting Your NXT_G Program

The last stage in the development of Alarm Bot is to document the NXT-G program through the addition of comments that explain the program's purpose and operation. This is easily accomplished through the addition of the comments shown in Figure 12.29.

That's everything! Before you put this book down and move on to other things, spend a little more time playing with and testing the operation of Alarm Bot. Once you are confident that everything works correctly, show it off to your family and friends.

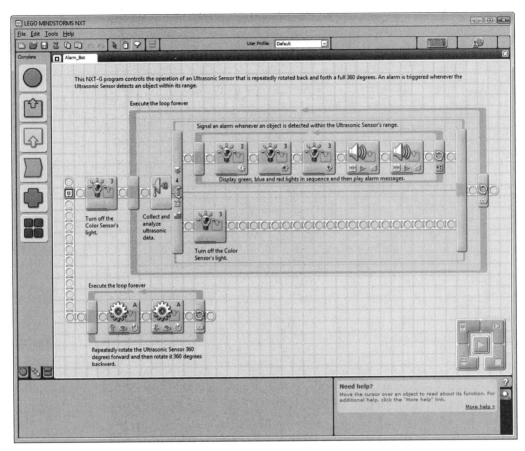

Figure 12.29
The final version of the Alarm_Bot NXT-G program.

SUMMARY

In this chapter, you learned how to create the book's final robot development project, Alarm Bot. This robot sounds an alarm whenever it detects an object within four feet of it. In doing so, you gained practical experience working with the ultrasonic sensor, which is mounted on top of an 8M cross axle and repeatedly rotated a full 360 degrees in order to allow the robot to detect intruders approaching from any direction. You also learned how to work with the color sensor as a lamp, displaying a series of different colored lights whenever an intruder is detected and the alarm is sounded.

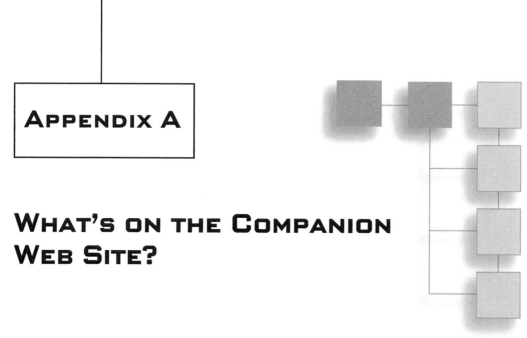

APPENDIX A

WHAT'S ON THE COMPANION WEB SITE?

Congratulations on making it all the way to the end of this book. At this point you should have a solid understanding of how to use Lego Mindstorms NXT 2.0 to create and program all kinds of exciting robotic creations. With this foundation now in place, you are well positioned to continue the development of your robotic design and program development skills.

There is plenty left to learn, so don't look at completing this book as the end of your education, but rather consider it to be the beginning. To join the ranks of advanced robotic developers, you need to keep learning everything you can about Lego Mindstorms NXT 2.0, and most importantly, you need to keep experimenting and building all kinds of new robotic creations. The only limit to what you can do is your own imagination.

As you continue to experiment and try your hand with different robotic creations, you will amass quite an inventory of creation and NXT-G source code. You can use the designs and source code that you create as the basis for even more complex and challenging creations. This way, you can borrow design ideas and source code and use them to model new creations based on existing ones. This will save you a lot of time, sweat, and tears because you won't have to reinvent the wheel every time you begin a new development project.

Assuming that you have re-created all of the robotic creations that have been presented in this book, you should already have a lot of good experience designing and programming your creations. You should faithfully document and add to this collection every time you create a new project. You'll come to appreciate the advantages and time savings from practicing this habit and will come to view these resources as indispensible.

Downloading the Book's Source Code

This book is most effectively used when you take the time to re-create all of its development examples. The hands-on experience that you gain by doing this will greatly improve your working knowledge of robotic development. However, in the event you did not have the time to re-create every example that was presented, you can download the missing project source code for these projects from the book's companion web page, located at http://www.courseptr.com/ downloads. Of course, to use them you'll need to re-create their robotic counterparts or modify the source code to meet the needs of some new project.

Table A.1 provides a brief explanation of the development projects that you will find on the companion web site.

Table A.1 Source Code Available on the Companion Web Site

Chapter	Program File
Chapter 9	Go_Bot.rbt
Chapter 10	Tracker_Bot.rbt
Chapter 11	Detect_Bot.rbt
Chapter 12	Alarm_Bot.rbt

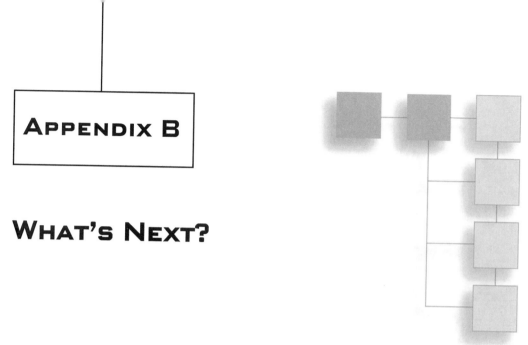

APPENDIX B

WHAT'S NEXT?

As you no doubt have learned, robotic development and programming are not only challenging but a whole lot of fun. While this book has taught you a lot about Lego Mindstorms NXT 2.0 and how to use it to develop all sorts of robotic creations, there is a lot more to this development framework than can possibly be covered in any one book. The purpose of this appendix is to provide you with a collection of online resources to which you can turn for more information about Lego Mindstorms NXT 2.0. In addition, you will find resources listed for Lego in general and LDraw, the CAD (Computer Aided Design) software used in this book to generate 3D images and design instructions. With it, you can create documentation for your own robotic creations.

LOCATING LEGO MINDSTORMS RESOURCES ONLINE

There is a lot of information about Lego Mindstorms NXT 2.0 available on the Internet if you know where to look for it. To help you get started, this appendix provides you with a list of essential web sites that you should frequent regularly in order to keep abreast of the latest information on Lego, Lego Mindstorms NXT 2.0, and LDraw.

The Lego Mindstorms Web Site

The official Lego Mindstorms web page is located at http://mindstorms.lego. com, as shown in Figure B.1. This site provides extensive information on Lego

Figure B.1
The Lego Mindstorms web site provides information and hosts activities and communication for a global community of Mindstorms enthusiasts.

Mindstorms NXT 2.0. You can sign up for a free Lego Mindstorms newsletter and participate in different building challenges. You can watch short movies, view fan-built projects, post and read questions and answers on forums, and even download free sounds for use in your projects.

The Open Directory Project's Mindstorms Page

Another excellent source for information on Lego Mindstorms NXT 2.0 is the Mindstorms web page at the open directory project, located at http://www.dmoz

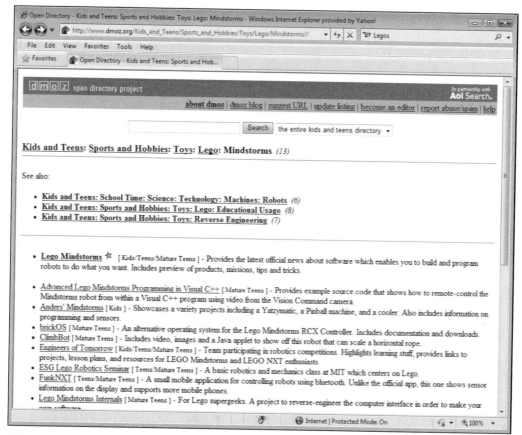

Figure B.2
The Mindstorms page at the open directory project.

.org/Kids_and_Teens/Sports_and_Hobbies/Toys/Lego/Mindstorms//, as shown in Figure B.2. Here you will find links to all kinds of topics.

The NXT Step—Lego Mindstorms NXT Blog

Another great way of keeping abreast of the latest happenings with Lego Mindstorms NXT 2.0 is to regularly visit the NXT Step—Lego Mindstorms NXT Blog available at http://thenxtstep.blogspot.com/ as shown in Figure B.3.

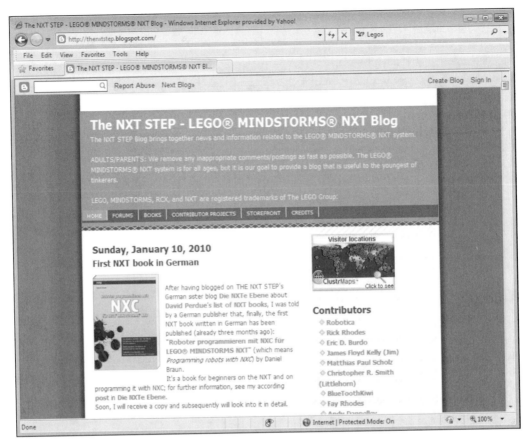

Figure B.3
This blog facilitates an ongoing global conversation for Lego Mindstorms NXT enthusiasts.

The site also provides access to the NXT STEP Forum, where you can participate in a host of different types of discussions.

The nxtprograms.com Web Site

The nxtprograms.com web site, shown in Figure B.4, provides you with access to instructions for building all kinds of robotic creations. Each project comes

Figure B.4
Visit this site to get free instructions for building all kinds of different robots.

complete with color building instructions. You can even download the programs needed to bring these robots to life.

The Wikipedia Lego Mindstorms NXT 2.0 Page

The Wikipedia Lego Mindstorms NXT 2.0 page, shown in Figure B.5, is located at http://en.wikipedia.org/wiki/Lego_Mindstorms_NXT_2.0. It provides a good overview of Lego Mindstorms NXT 2.0 and is a great source of references and links to online content, including articles and links to other web sites.

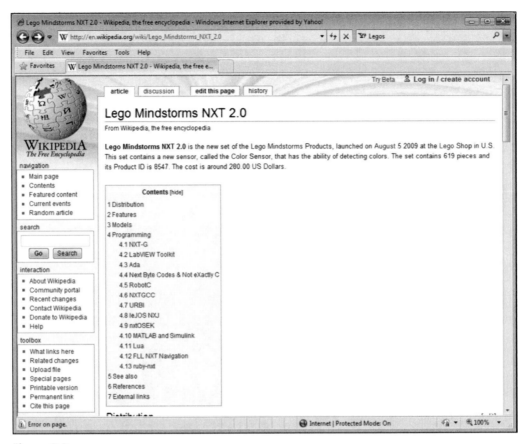

Figure B.5
The Wikipedia Lego Mindstorms page is developed and maintained by a worldwide community of robotic developers dedicated to sharing information.

The nxtasy.org Site

The nxtasy.org web site (http://nxtasy.org/), shown in Figure B.6, is dedicated to being a source of news and information exchange for Lego Mindstorms NXT users. It is rich with technical information and discussion. It also hosts different challenges—worldwide competitions that you can participate in. This site also hosts a forums area where you can post and read information shared among thousands of Lego Mindstorms enthusiasts.

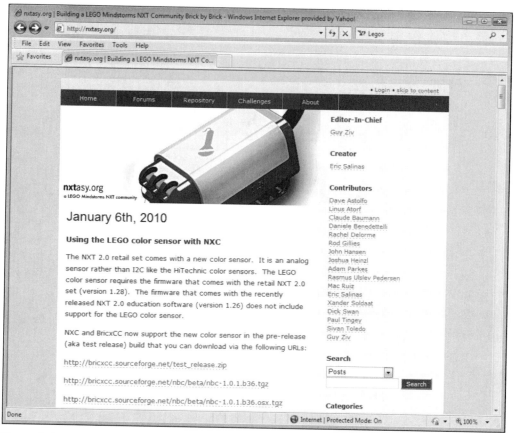

Figure B.6
Be sure to check out the Forums section at nxtasy.org.

BUY NEW LEGO MINDSTORMS NXT PARTS

If any of the electronic pieces belonging to your Lego Mindstorms NXT 2.0 kit break and need to be replaced or if you find yourself working on projects that require more electronic parts than came with the kit, you can purchase what you need from the Lego Shop located at http://shop.lego.com. Once there, do a search on Mindstorms and you'll see a listing of all available parts as demonstrated in Figure B.7. In addition, you can also purchase sensors not supplied with your kit. These sensors include the gyroscopic sensor, infrared sensor, accelerometer sensor, compass sensor, sound sensor, and light sensor.

Figure B.7
If you need more parts than came with your kit, you can buy them from the Lego Shop.

LEGO RESOURCES

While you can create untold number of robots using just the pieces and parts that come with the Lego Mindstorms NXT 2.0 kit, there is no reason for you to limit yourself to just these resources. If you want, you can incorporate other types of Lego blocks and pieces into your creations, further expanding the types of things you can build.

The Lego Web Site

While this book has provided you with a lot of good information on Lego Mindstorms NXT 2.0, it has not focused much on the rest of the Lego Universe,

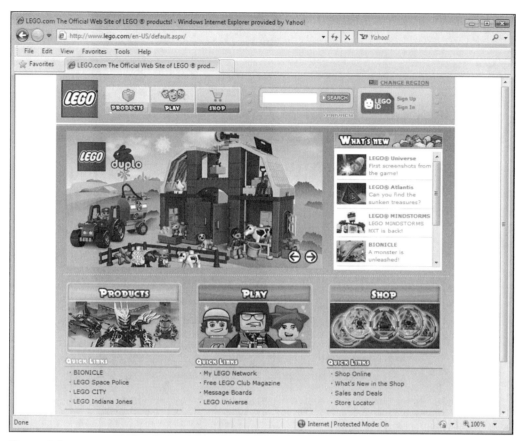

Figure B.8
There is no reason that you could not incorporate regular Lego blocks into your robotic creations.

which is amazingly extensive. To learn more about Lego, you should visit http://www.lego.com, as shown in Figure B.8. Here you will find information about Lego bricks, play sets, Mindstorms, and much more.

Lego Club

There is no better way to stay in touch with the greater Lego community than by joining the Lego Club, located at http://club.lego.com, as shown in Figure B.9.

Figure B.9
The Lego club is the place where Lego lovers around the world congregate and share information.

Here you can play games, post and read questions and answers on the site's message boards, and sign up for the free club magazine.

The Lego Page at Wikipedia

Another source of information for Lego is the Lego Page at Wikipedia (http://en. wikipedia.org/wiki/Lego (http://en.wikipedia.org/wiki/Lego), shown in Figure B.10. Here you will find historical information about Lego as well as references to tons of online resources and Lego books.

Figure B.10
Wikipedia's Lego page provides an excellent historical overview of Lego's origins.

DEVELOPING INSTRUCTIONS FOR YOUR ROBOTIC CREATIONS

If you want to document your own Lego robotic creations, one option is to use LDraw. LDraw is a free CAD-like software application that can be used to model Lego creations in 3D. Alternatively, you can use the LEGO Digital Designer program.

Wikipedia's LDraw Page

Wikipedia's LDraw page (http://en.wikipedia.org/wiki/Ldraw), shown in Figure B.11, provides an overview of LDraw. This site provides a good overview of the different software components that make up LDraw and provides information about books that cover LDraw.

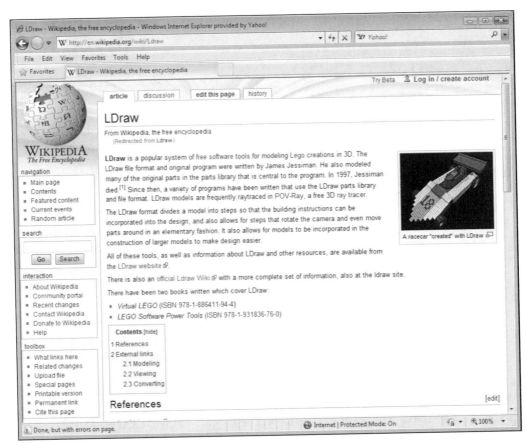

Figure B.11
Wikipedia's LDraw page provides a good overview of LDraw.

LDraw.org

LDraw's main web site is www.ldraw.org, as shown in Figure B.12. This site provides a history of LDraw and provides information about books, online resources, and all things LDraw. You can download and install LDraw from this site. Instructions are provided for installing LDraw. There are also tutorials that you can read to learn all about LDraw and its operation.

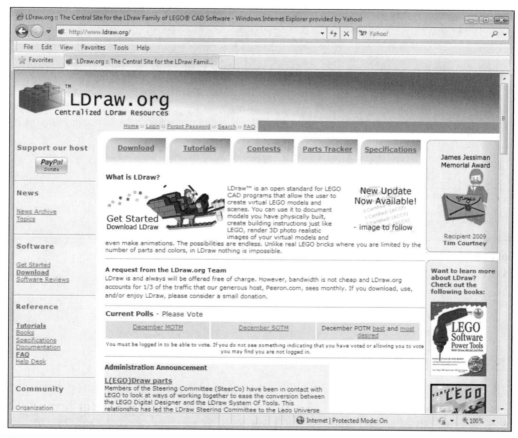

Figure B.12
LDraw.org is central headquarters for keeping up with all things related to LDraw.

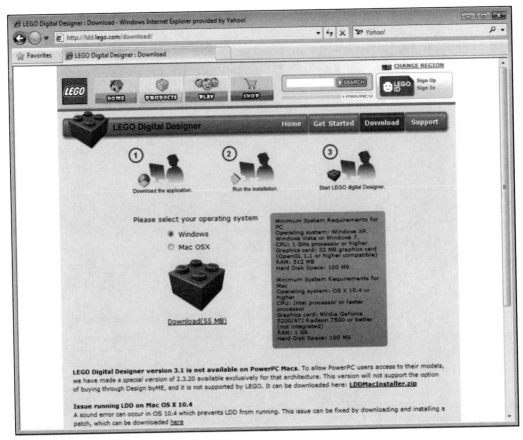

Figure B.13
LEGO Digital Designer is easy to install and operate.

LEGO Digital Designer

LEGO Digital Designer, or LDD, is a free CAD program developed by Lego Group. As shown in Figure B.13, you can download a copy of it at http://ldd. lego.com/download/. It works on both Microsoft Windows and Mac OS X.

THE AUTHOR'S WEB SITE

If you enjoyed this book and are interested in learning about other game developer options or other programming languages, visit my web site located at

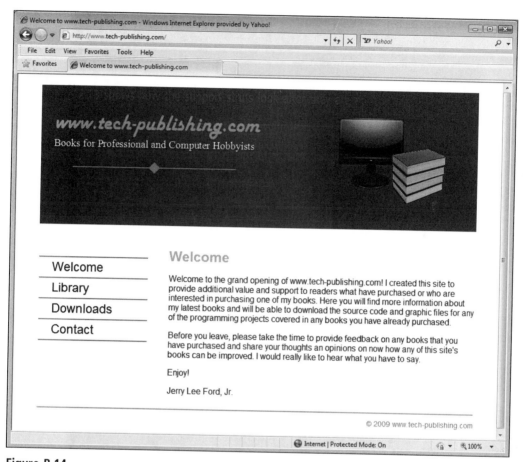

Figure B.14
Visit www.tech-publishing.com to learn more about game development and to provide your feedback on this book.

http://www.tech-publishing.com, as shown in Figure B.14. While you are there, drop me a message to let me know what you think of the book or how you think it might be improved.

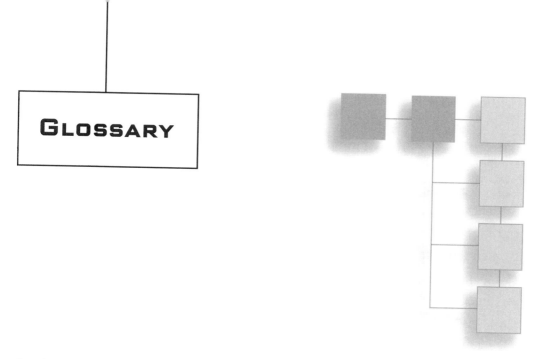

GLOSSARY

Angle Connector. Used to connect two axles and to create 90- or 180-degree connections.

Angular Beam. A beam in which one or more sections are angled.

Attributes. Programming block properties or modifiers that can be configured to customize the programming block's execution.

Axle. A cross-shaped shaft that can be used to connect to any Mindstorms piece that has a cross-hole connection.

Block Import and Export Wizard. A utility program that provides the ability to import new programming blocks and to export custom-developed programming blocks.

Bluetooth. A wireless networking technology that can be used to wirelessly download your NXT-G programs into the NXT Brick.

Bluetooth Connection Block. A programming block that establishes a connection to another Bluetooth device or disables/enables Bluetooth functionality.

Bushing. Used to hold an axle firmly in position, locking other pieces that may be connected to the axle in place.

Calibrate Block. A programming block that calibrates the minimum and maximum values detected by sound/light sensors.

Calibrate Sensors. A utility program that facilitates the re-calibration of sensors to tune their operations.

Catch with Cross-hole Connector. Connects axles that intersect perpendicularly.

Color Lamp Block. A programming block that controls the Color Sensor's lamp function, emitting red, green, or blue light.

Color Sensor. Provides robots with the ability to detect different colors and light, and to generate light.

Color Sensor Block. A programming block that enables the detection of different colors and the measurement of light intensity.

Comb Wheel. Connects up to four axles and can be used in various ways, as a stabilizer for axles or as an attachment that extends the effects of gears.

Comments. Text strings added to NXT-G programs for the purpose of documenting the programs.

Common Palette. A tab on the Programming palette that contains the most commonly used programming blocks.

Compare Block. A programming block that determines if a number is greater than, less than, or equal to another number.

Complete Palette. A tab on the Programming palette that provides access to all programming blocks.

Conditional Logic. The process of executing sets of programming blocks based on whether or not a tested value evaluates as true.

Configuration Panel. A window that displays and allows you to customize the operation of the programming block, modifying both input and output and other attributes and actions.

Conical Gear. A gear whose teeth are shaped to allow them to mesh with one another when mounted on a parallel axis or when mounted perpendicular to one another.

Connector. Allows you to connect and tie together different Mindstorms pieces into a cohesive whole.

Constant Block. A programming block that returns a value stored in a constant.

Create Pack and Go. A utility program that creates a Pack and Go file facilitating development functions like My Blocks, Display Blocks, and Sound Blocks with other NXT developers.

Cross Axle Extension. Connects two axles in order to establish a longer axle.

Cross Block. A Lego Mindstorms NXT 2.0 piece that combines circular and cross-hole connections.

Custom Palette. A tab on the Programming palette that provides access to blocks that you create or upload into Mindstorms NXT 2.0.

Data. A piece of information collected, stored, modified, and processed during application execution.

Data Hub. A projection that slides down from the bottom left side of a programming block which contains one or more data plugs that allow the programming block to send and receive data.

Data Wire. A connection between one block's output data plug and another block's input data plug.

Developer Profile. An organizational mechanism whereby NXT-G programmers are only presented with programs that they develop.

Display Block. A programming block that displays text, shapes, and images on the NXT Brick's LCD.

Driven Gear. The last gear in the gear train.

Driver Gear. The gear that is responsible for transferring motion to the other gears in a gear train.

Endless Loop. A loop that does not have a predefined means of terminating its own execution.

File Access Block. A programming block that saves data to files on your NXT Brick.

FIRST LEGO League (FLL). A worldwide robotic design competition started in 1999 for the purpose of getting children interested in science and technology.

Flexible Axle Damper 2M Connector. Connects axles that run in parallel; supports robotic creations that require flexibility.

Flow. The order in which program blocks are executed within a NXT-G program.

Flowchart. A graphical depiction of some or all of a program's logic.

Friction Peg. A peg that firmly holds its position within a round hole.

Gear. Used to transmit motion (five different types of gears).

Gear Ratio. Describes the rotation of the driver gear relative to the driven gear.

Gear Train. The use of two or more gears together.

Gearing Down. Occurs when you either decrease the size of the driver gear or increase the size of the driven gear.

Gearing Up. Occurs when you either increase the size of the driver gear or reduce the size of the driven gear.

IDE (Integrated Development Environment). A graphical application development environment designed to facilitate program development.

Idler Gear. Gears located between the driver gear and the driven gear in a great train.

Image Editor. A utility program that lets you convert and download graphic files onto your NXT Brick, where they can then be loaded and displayed on the Brick's LCD screen.

Input Data Plug. Used to accept data passed to the programming blocks.

Integrated Development Environment (IDE). A collection of computer programs that execute from a single user interface.

Keep Alive Block. A programming block that prevents the NXT Brick from going to sleep.

Knob Gear. A gear with four circular knobs that rotate around its axis.

Lego Mindstorms NXT. A robotics kit developed by Lego in 2006, which was the predecessor to the Lego Mindstorms 2.0 kit.

Lego Mindstorms NXT 2.0. A robotics kit developed by Lego in August 2009.

Light Sensor Block. A programming block that detects ambient light.

Liquid Crystal Display (LCD). A monochrome display on the NXT Brick that is 100 pixels wide by 64 pixels high.

Little Help Window. Displays information about the currently selected object as well as a link to additional information about the object in the Lego Mindstorms NXT 2.0 help file.

Logic Block. A programming block that reviews inputs and returns a true/false value.

Logic Data. A term used to represent data that has either of two values: true or false.

Loop. A collection of one or more programming blocks that are repeatedly executed.

Loop Block. A programming block that repeats the execution of specified programming blocks.

Magazine. Holds balls for using with robots that shoot.

Math Block. A programming block that performs arithmetic, subtraction, multiplication, and division operations.

Mesh. The interlocking of gear teeth that facilitates the transference of motion between gears.

Microcomputer. A small digital computer designed to be used by one person at a time.

Module. A unit of measurement (8mm) that is used to identify the length of beams and other parts.

Motor Block. A programming block that provides precise control of a motor's speed.

Move Block. A programming block that moves a robotic creation forward or backward.

My Block. A collection of one or more customized programming blocks that perform a specific task.

My Portal. A window that provides a gateway to the http://www.mindstorms.com web site, providing access to information on new models, program files, and sound and image files.

Number to Text Block. A programming block that takes a number and turns it into a displayable text string.

NXT Brick. A programmable microcomputer that controls the operations of robotic creations.

NXT Buttons Block. A programming block that sends true value through a data wire whenever a NXT button is activated.

NXT Controller. A utility program that transfers program and data files to your NXT Brick, starts and stops NXT-G programs, and changes NXT Brick settings.

NXT-G. The programming language supplied by Lego for developing programs that execute on the NXT Brick.

NXT-G Program. A computer program created by dragging and dropping different programming blocks onto the work area. Every new NXT-G program starts out with a Starting Point sequence beam.

NXT Window. Manages NXT Brick memory and connections to the NXT Brick.

Output Data Plug. Used to pass data to other programming blocks.

Peg. Connects beams and other types of pieces that have holes.

Peg Block. A highly specialized type of peg that combines features of beams and pegs, having circular holes that run in multiple directions, facilitating parallel and perpendicular connections.

Programming Blocks. The basic building blocks used to outline the programming logic that makes up a NXT-G program.

Programming Palette. The windows on which programming blocks are stored and organized.

Pseudo Code. An English-like outline of some or all of the logic involved in the development of a computer program.

Random Block. A programming block that generates a random number.

Range Block. A programming block that determines whether a number is inside a range of numbers.

RCX. A microcomputer supplied with the Robotics Invention System (RIS).

Receive Message Block. A programming block that enables the receipt of wireless messages.

Record/Play Block. A programming block that records an action manually performed with a robotic creation and then allows that action to be replayed.

Remote Control. A utility program that allows you to control your robotic creations from your computer, controlling both speed and direction.

Reset Motor Block. A programming block that disables the automatic error correction for servo motors.

Rim. Attaches directly to axles and transfers motion passed through axles to either tires or tracks.

RJ12 Connector. A cable used to connect a sensor or servo motor to the NXT Brick.

Robo Center. An IDE window that provides access to building instructions for creating different types of robots.

Robotics Invention System (RIS). A robotics kit developed by Lego in 1998.

Rotation Sensor Block. A programming block that counts the number of degrees or the number of rotations that a motor turns.

Send Message Block. A programming block that is used to send a wireless message to your NXT Brick via a Bluetooth connection.

Sequence Beams. Connectors used in the formulation of NXT-G programs that allow programming blocks to be connected to the Starting Point.

Servo Motor. Provides robots with the ability to move and grasp things.

Shooter. Provides a means of shooting balls.

Smooth Peg. A peg that moves freely within round holes.

Sound Block. A programming block that instructs the NXT Brick to play a sound file.

Sound Editor. A utility program that allows you to convert sound files on your computer into a format supported by the NXT Brick.

Sound Sensor Block. A programming block that detects sounds and reports on sound level.

Starting Point. An object located on the left side of the work area that marks the beginning of all NXT-G programs.

Steering Link. Establishes a connection with either the friction ball peg or the smooth axle ball peg.

Stop Block. A programming block that halts program execution and any running motors.

Stop Ridge. A notch on an axle or peg that determines how far an axle or peg can go into a hole.

Straight Beam. A Lego Mindstorms NXT 2.0 piece that is perforated with circular holes which run down the middle of the beam and which has a smooth exterior and rounded ends.

String. A set of characters that can be passed between programming blocks and displayed on the NXT Brick's LCD.

Switch Block. A programming block that chooses between two alternate courses of action based on the analysis of sensor or input value.

T-Beam. A beam that is T-shaped and is 3M wide and 3M tall.

Tachometer. A component within a sensor motor that precisely controls the rotation of the motors.

Text Block. A programming block that adds text strings together in order to create a longer text string.

Timer Block. A programming block that reads the timer's current value or restarts the timer.

Tire. Used to create cars and any other type of wheeled vehicle or machine (tires are made to fit snuggly around the rims).

Touch Sensor. Provides robots with a sense of touch, allowing them to feel and react to things around them.

Touch Sensor Block. A programming block that sends a true/false signal through a data wire based on the current condition of a touch sensor.

Track. Ribbed rubber banks used to make things like tanks, construction vehicles, and other machines.

Ultrasonic Sensor. Provides robots with the ability to see objects and to determine their distance.

Ultrasonic Sensor Block. A programming block that establishes a connection to another Bluetooth device.

Update NXT Firmware. A utility program that provides the ability to update the NXT Brick's firmware to the most current version, allowing you to take advantage of any improvements made by Lego.

Variable. A location in memory where an individual piece of data is stored.

Variable Block. A programming block that reads or writes variable values.

V Belt. A small rubber band that can be used to loosely bind pieces together.

Wait Block. A programming block that pauses NXT-G program execution.

Web Block. A My Block that someone else has developed and which you have downloaded from the Internet.

Work Area. The large, gray, gridded area where NXT-G programs are defined.

Work Area Map. Allows you to quickly navigate the work area by clicking and holding down the left mouse button on any area within the work area map window and then move the cursor to a new area.

INDEX